" Simply
SHOOTERS "

a.k.a
COAST TO COAST
SHOOTER
COLLECTION

THE
PROFESSIONAL
BARTENDER'S
DIRECTORY

BY
EUGENE COOLIK
© **JUST BEVERAGE PUBLICATIONS**

OTHER BOOKS BY EUGENE COOLIK

Bartender's Little Black Book: First Edition
Thinking Professionally Has Its Own Rewards: An Essay

JUST BEVERAGE PUBLICATIONS

" *Simply* SHOOTERS"

a.k.a
COAST TO COAST
SHOOTER
COLLECTION

TABLE OF CONTENTS

DEDICATION

Dedicated to Joe Argush, my instructor at Georgia School of Bartending, Atlanta – so, so many years ago. Wherever you are Joe, I hope life has been good to you! E.C.

ACKNOWLEDGEMENTS

To all cocktail recipe book writers, bartending schools, bars, lounges, nightclubs and restaurants, etc., both chains and privately owned, thank you for putting into print all these shooters. And thanks to all of you loyal shooter drinkers out there for ordering, drinking and keeping alive all the popular recipes found within these pages.
Happy Shooting!

INTRODUCTION

Within the covers of **"SIMPLY SHOOTERS"** you will find **over 1150 legitimate shooter recipes.** This researcher and compiler has sifted and sorted through **over 75 publications,** books, recipe lists and files from throughout the country and selected only the ones considered shooters that are regularly and consistently ordered in bars across the U.S.A. and Canada. This writer sincerely hopes the professional bartender will be helped through this completed endeavor, **"COAST TO COAST SHOOTER COLLECTION."**

PLEASE TAKE NOTE

The compiler of these recipes hopes that no one is offended by any shooter names appearing in this book. You may detect that in some cases drink names have been slightly altered for this very reason. Though some may seem a bit "off color" and even lean toward vulgar, it would render this specialty recipe book lacking had any of these shooters/drinks been excluded. The intention of this book is to provide the most popular and widely known shooters, by name and recipe, to the professional mixologist and American drinking public. E.C.

REALLY, WHAT IS A SHOOTER?

DEFINITION.........Any miniature cocktail ordered and prepared with the intention of being consumed rapidly, usually in one to three gulps. The shooter evolved from a combination of the unsophisticated "shot" of whiskey and the very proper "pousse cafe´," a French style miniature after dinner cocktail created to be sipped with coffee. The wide popularity and rapid acceptance of this new category of cocktails is unprecedented in alcohol beverage history. One of the first "shooters" may have simply been 1 ounce of Peppermint Schnapps served neat (without ice) in a Dutch cordial glass at Clarence Foster's or Harrison's on Peachtree. With the onset of the Vietnam War and the resultant reduction of the legal drinking age, there was a huge explosion of new cocktails (leading to shooters) with diverse names and ingredients that has not yet ended and will most likely reach into the next century.

INGREDIENTS.........Any combination of liqueur (cordial), liquor, syrup, fruit juice, cream, whipped cream and even wine, beer or carbonated beverage.

MIXING METHODS.........There are several ways these drinks are prepared. See the following.

Shake and Strain – This requires either a metal shaker can and mixing glass or a blender/mixer. Pour ingredients over ice, shake 6 or 7 times using metal shaker and glass or "flash" blend two or three seconds if using a blender/mixer, and strain (holding ice back) into the proper (chilled) glass.

Blend – To prepare "Shluuters" – (Slushy Shooters) – use crushed ice, pour ingredients into blender canister and blend until "slushy." Serve these shooters promptly!

Build/Pour – These instructions dictate that ingredients should be poured from the bottle into the proper serving glass – with or without ice as the recipe or customer indicate. A quick stir or swirl may be in order.

Layer/Float – First of all, the proof of all liqueurs, cordials and liquors must be taken into consideration. Based upon Bolsweight and Specific Gravity Indexes – the higher the index number the higher (heavier) the density (weight) of the liqueur. When the charts give the proofs they are most always shown to be <u>low proof</u> equals <u>heavy weight</u>, <u>high proof</u> equals <u>lighter weight</u>. Therefore, the saying goes, "The lower the proof the heavier the weight (density), consequently the lower the liqueur settles (sits) in the glass." The opposite holds true for the higher proof liqueurs and liquors. "The higher the proof the lighter the weight (density) and the higher it floats or layers on the other heavier ingredients." In layering, the heavier, lowest proof ingredient is first poured. The second ingredient is then gently allowed to flow over the back of a small spoon, cherry, inverted round headed stir stick or several sip sticks held together so as to force its flow to the side of the glass and spread out upon the previously poured heavier ingredient. Continue in this manner with all ingredients when layering a shooter. Be aware that not all distilleries use the same formulas (recipes) and even though something is 50 proof it may not be in fact heavier than something 60 proof. <u>Be sure that you use cordials with more than several degrees difference in proofs.</u>

GLASSWARE.........The glassware is of course part of establishment (house) policy. <u>See the following.</u>

<u>Shake and Strain/Stir and Strain</u> drinks should be served in chilled rocks (stemmed or flat based) or chilled cocktail glasses. Smaller glassware is also often used.

Build/Pour procedure will usually require a rocks glass or possibly a large shot/shooter glass, with or without ice, according to the recipe or customer request.

Layered and Floated shooters and pousse cafes´ are prepared in a cordial/liqueur/pony/shooter or Dutch cordial glass. Many bars also use a shot or small rocks glass for this type of drink. Be aware of ever increasing popularity of test tubes and speciality shooter glassware.

FLAMING.........This book, author and publisher, consider flaming dangerous and do not recommend the practice of igniting any shooter or pousse cafe´ and therefore offer no instructions to do so. Check with your house policy before flaming drinks. **"Let common sense prevail."**

REMINDER # 1.........With shooters, please remember all the possible variations, modifications, changes and renditions to the ingredients, names and mixing methods that do occur. The recipes in this book may easily be changed in quantities, mixing method and glassware at the customer's request, but remember, when we use more or less alcohol, we charge more or less for the shooter. **The price changes!** House policy is boss and should set all pricing guidelines.

REMINDER # 2.........We mixologists are dispensing potent drinks and should be monitoring our guests for over-consumption. If signs of intoxication are detected, we slow down or discontinue service of alcohol. Food and non-alcoholic drinks are offered. **We strive to be part of the solution rather than part of the problem.** Remember **"over the limit and behind the wheel"** may cause laws to be broken and attract **"blue-lights."** Call a cab – call a friend, remember, **responsible alcohol beverage service** has its own rewards and the guest may even thank us later! E.C.

"Simply SHOOTERS"

SHOOTER TOASTS IN DIFFERENT COUNTRIES

Australia	Cheers!
Bermuda	Cheers!
Brazil	Asuasaude!
Canada	Cheers!
China	Kan Pei!
Denmark	Skal!
England	Cheers!
Finland	Kippis!
France	A Votre Sante!
Germany	Prosit!
Greece	Stin Ygia Sou!
Hawaii	Kamaul!
Hungary	Egeszegedre!
Iceland	Skal!
Ireland	Slainte is Saol Agat!
Israel	L'Chaim!
Italy	Alla Tua Salute!
Jamaica	Cheers!
Japan	Kan Pai!
Mexico	Salud!
Morocco	Sahrtek!
Nassau	Cheers!
New Zealand	Cheers!
Norway	Skal!
Philippines	Mabuhay!
Poland	Nazdrowie!
Portugal	A Sua Saude!
Romania	Noroc!
Russia	Za Vashe Zdorovye!
Saudi Arabia	Hanian!
Scotland	Slaint Mhoiz!
Singapore	Yam Seng!
South Africa	Cheers!
Spain	Salud!
Sweden	Skal!
Tiawan	Kan Pei!
Turkey	Serefinize!
United States	Cheers!
Virgin Islands	Cheers!
Yugoslavia	Ziveli!

"Cheers" "Salute" "To Your Health" "To Life" "Bottoms Up" "Congratulations" "Good Luck" "Success To You" "To Your Honor" "A Salute To You" "To The Good Life" "Be Well" "Long Life" "All The Best" "Here's To You" "Just Be Happy" "Here's How" "To Peace Forever"

"Simply SHOOTERS"

IMPORTANT INFORMATION

PLEASE TAKE NOTE

"Stop The Press"
Drink Addendum
Recipes From
Page 123-129

RE-ORDER FORMS

Order For
Friends, Family
Your Fellow
Bartenders
and Cocktail
Servers
See Last Page

HOPING YOU FIND

The Print Size
And Format An
Ease In The
Sometimes Dim
Bar Lighting

BE SURE THAT

You Use The
Added Extra
Pages 130-140
For All Your
New Shooter
Recipes

"Simply
SHOOTERS"

AAA TRAVEL CLUB
Shake and Strain
- 1/2 oz Amaretto
- 1/2 oz Apple Schnapps
- 1/2 oz Apricot Brandy

A AND B
Layer
Kahlua
Bailey's Irish Cream
151° Rum
Flaming not recommended

ABC
Layer
Amaretto
Bailey's Irish Cream
Cointreau

A BOMB I
Shake and Strain
- 1/2 oz Kahlua
- 1/2 oz Bailey's Irish Cream
- 1/2 oz Vodka
- 1/4 oz Grand Marnier
- 1/4 oz Tia Maria

A BOMB II
Layer
Kahlua
Bailey's Irish Cream
151° Rum
Flaming not recommended

ABSOLUT NUT
Shake and Strain
- 1 oz Frangelico
- 1 oz Absolut Vodka

ABSOLUT QUAALUDE
Shake and Strain
- 1 oz Frangelico
- 1 oz Bailey's Irish Cream
- 1 oz Absolut Vodka

ABURGOUT
In a Rocks Glass
- 1/4 oz Brandy
- Float Peppermint Schnapps

ACCELERATOR
Build, No Ice, Rocks Glass
Drink Quickly
- 1 oz Vodka
- 1 oz Peppermint Schnapps
- 1 oz Cherry Brandy

AFRICAN VIOLET
Layer
G. Creme de Menthe
Frangelico

AFTER BURNER
Shake and Strain
- 1 1/4 oz Peppermint Schnapps
- 3/4 oz Tia Maria

"Simply
SHOOTERS"

AFTER EIGHT
Layer
Bailey's Irish Cream
Kahlua
W. Creme de Menthe

AFTER FIVE
Layer
Kahlua
Bailey's Irish Cream
Peppermint Schnapps

AFTER SIX
Layer
Kahlua
Bailey's Irish Cream
Peppermint Schnapps
Vodka

AGENT 99
Layer
Parfait Amour
Anisette
Grand Marnier

AGENT ORANGE
Layer
Grand Marnier
151° Rum
Flaming not recommended

ALABAMA SLAMMER I
Southern Comfort
Sloe Gin
Orange Juice

ALABAMA SLAMMER II
Shake and Strain
1 oz Amaretto
1 oz Southern Comfort
1/2 oz Rose's
Lime Juice
1/2 oz Grenadine

ALABAMA SLAMMER (SHOOTER)
Shake and Strain
1/2 oz Southern Comfort
1/2 oz Amaretto
1/2 oz Sloe Gin
Splash Orange Juice
Splash Sour Mix

ALASKA LIGHTS
Layer
Kahlua
Brandy
Amaretto
Tequila
Flaming not recommended

ALASKA OILSPILL
Layer
Rumple Minze
Jagermeister

ALFONSO
Layer
W. Creme de Cacao
Cream

A

ALICE BANANALESS
Shake and Strain
- 1/2 oz Vodka
- 1/2 oz Amaretto
- 1/2 oz Midori
- 1/2 oz Cream

ALICE FROM DALLAS
Layer
- Kahlua
- Grand Marnier
- Tequila
- *Flaming not recommended*

ALICE IN WONDERLAND
Shake and Strain
- 3/4 oz Tequila
- 3/4 oz Grand Marnier
- 3/4 oz Drambuie

ALIEN
- D. Creme de Cacao
- Bailey's Irish Cream
- Cherry Brandy

ALLIGATOR
Shake and Strain
- 1/2 oz Apple Schnapps
- 1/2 oz Midori
- 1/2 oz Blended Whiskey
- Splash Sour Mix

AMARIST (AMERIS)
Snifter, No Ice
- 3/4 oz Amaretto
- 3/4 oz Grand Marnier

AMBUSHED
Shake and Strain
- 1 oz Old Bushmills
- 1 oz Amaretto

AMERICAN DREAM
Layer
- Kahlua
- Chocolate Schnapps
- Frangelico

AMERICA'S FLAG FLIES
Layer
- Grenadine
- Blue Curacao
- Half & Half

AMIGO
Shake and Strain
- 3/4 oz Tequila
- 3/4 oz Kahlua
- Splash Cream
- Sprinkle Nutmeg

AMOUR POUSSE
Layer
- Grenadine
- Maraschino
- Brandy
- *Flaming not recommended*

ANESTHESIZER
Layer
- Peppermint Schnapps
- Canadian Whisky

ANGEL'S BLISS
Layer
Wild Turkey Liqueur
Blue Curacao
Rum 151°
Flaming not recommended

ANGEL'S BREATH
Layer
D. Creme de Cacao
Irish Cream
Cherry on Top

ANGEL'S DELIGHT
Layer
Grenadine
Triple Sec
Creme Yvette
Cream

ANGEL'S KISS
Layer
D. Creme de Cacao
Creme Yvette
Brandy
Cream

ANGEL'S LIPS
B&B
Cream

ANGEL'S TIP
B. Creme de Cacao
Cream
Cherry Garnish

ANGEL'S WING
Layer
W. Creme de Cacao
Brandy
Cream

ANTI-FREEZE I
Shake and Strain
Midori, Gin
Orange Juice
Sour Mix

ANTI-FREEZE II
Layer
Parfait Amour
Blue Curacao

APPLE BALL
Shake and Strain
1 1/4 oz Apple
Schnapps
Splash Gingerale

APPLE JACK
Layer
Apple Schnapps
Jack Daniels

APPLE MINT
Shake and Strain
1 1/4 Apple Schnapps
3/4 oz Peppermint
Schnapps

APPLE MINTZ
Shake and Strain
1 1/4 oz Apple Schnapps
3/4 oz Rumple Mintz Schnapps

APPLE PIE
Layer
Apple Schnapps
Cinnamon Schnapps
Bailey's Irish Cream (Optional)

APPLES AND SPICE
Shake and Strain
1 1/4 oz Apple Schnapps
1/4 oz Cinnamon Schnapps
Splash Cream

ARBURGHOUT
Peppermint Schnapps
Brandy
Flaming not recommended

ARMADILLO
Layer
Parfait Amour
Tia Maria
Cream

ASSASSIN
Layer
Banana Liqueur
Blue Curacao
Grand Marnier

ATTITUDE ADJUSTMENT
Layer
Bailey's Irish Cream
Rootbeer Schnapps
Southern Comfort

AUGUST MOON
Layer
Triple Sec
Amaretto
Orange Juice
Whipped Cream

AUNT JEMIMA
W. Creme de Cacao
Benedictine
Brandy

AVALANCHE
Layer
Kahlua
W. Creme de Menthe
Southern Comfort

AVIATION
Shake and Strain
3/4 oz Harvey's Bristol Cream
3/4 oz Dubonnet (Red)

B-12
Layer
   Bailey's Irish Cream
   Grand Marnier

B-50
Layer
   Vodka
   Bailey's Irish Cream

B-51
Layer
   Kahlua
   Bailey's Irish Cream
   Bacardi 151° Rum
   Flaming not recommended

B-52
Layer
   Kahlua
   Bailey's Irish Cream
   Grand Marnier

B-52 BOMBER
   Kahlua
   Bailey's Irish Cream
   Mandarine Napoleon

B-52 ON A MISSION
Layer
   Kahlua
   Bailey's Irish Cream
   Grand Marnier
   151° Rum
   Flaming not recommended

B-52/100
Layer
   Kahlua
   Bailey's Irish Cream
   Grand Marnier
   100° Vodka
   Flaming not recommended

B-53
   B-52 with Amaretto

B-53 ON FIRE
Layer
   Kahlua
   Bailey's Irish Cream
   Grand Marnier
   Bacardi 151°
   Flaming not recommended

B-57
Layer
   Kahlua
   Bailey's Irish Cream
   Grand Marnier
   Stolichnaya

B&B
Snifter, No Ice
   Brandy (Cognac)
   Benedictine

BABE RUTH
Layer
   Frangelico
   Vodka
   2 or 3 Peanuts

BABY BABY BABY
Shake and Strain
- 3/4 oz Vodka
- 3/4 oz Grand Marnier
- 3/4 oz Bailey's

BAD STING
Layer
- Grenadine
- Anisette
- Grand Marnier
- Tequila
Flaming not recommended

BAHAMA NUT
Layer
- 1/2 Nassau Royale
- 1/2 Frangelico

BAILEY'S COMET
Layer
- D. Creme de Cacao
- Amaretto
- Bailey's

BAJA BLUE SUEDE SHOOTER
Shake and Strain
- 1/2 oz Blueberry Schnapps
- 1/2 oz Malibu
- 1/2 oz Blue Curacao
- 1/2 oz Pineapple Juice

BALL BEARING
Layer
- Cherry Marnier
- Champagne

BANANA BOAT
Shake and Strain
- 1/2 oz Kahlua
- 1/2 oz Peppermint Schnapps
- 1/2 oz Bailey's
- 1/2 oz Banana Liqueur

BANANA BOOMER
Shake and Strain
- 3/4 oz Vodka
- 3/4 oz Banana Liqueur

BANANA NUTBREAD
Shake and Strain
- 3/4 oz Banana Liqueur
- 3/4 oz Frangelico
- 3/4 oz Bailey's Irish Cream

BANANA POPSICLE
Shake and Strain
- 3/4 oz Vodka
- 3/4 oz Creme de Banana
- Splash Orange Juice

BANANA PUDDING
Shake and Strain
- 3/4 oz Banana Liqueur
- 1/2 oz Kahlua
- 1/2 oz D. Creme de Cacao
- 1/2 oz Bailey's

B

BANANA SANDWICH
Layer
Kahlua
Banana Liqueur
Myers's Rum Cream

BANANA SPLIT I
Layer
Kahlua
Banana Liqueur
Creme de Noyaux
Cream

BANANA SPLIT II
Layer
Grenadine
Kahlua
Banana Liqueur
Whipped Cream
Cherry Garnish

BANANA SPLIT III
Shake and Strain
3/4 oz D. Creme de Cacao
3/4 oz Creme de Banana
3/4 oz Triple Sec
Splash Cream

BARBADOS BOMBER
Stir and Strain
1 1/2 oz Mount Gay Rum
1/2 oz Rose's Lime Juice
Dash Triple Sec

BARNEMINT BAILEY
Layer
Bailey's Irish Cream
W. Creme de Cacao
Cream

BAYOU
Layer
Kahlua
Bailey's Irish Cream
Midori

BAZOOKA
Shake and Strain
1 1/4 oz Southern
Comfort
3/4 oz. Banana Liqueur
Dash Grenadine
Splash Cream

BEACH BUM
Shake and Strain
1 oz Vodka
1/2 oz Midori
1/2 oz Pineapple Juice

BEACHCOMBER
Shake and Strain
1 1/4 oz Rum
1/2 oz Triple Sec
1/2 oz Rose's Lime Juice
Splash Grenadine

BEAM ME UP SCOTTY
Layer
  Kahlua
  Banana Liqueur
  Bailey's Irish Cream

BEAR GLUE
Layer
  Amaretto
  Vodka
  Flaming not recommended

BEAR HUG
Layer
  Kahlua
  Sambuca
  Grand Marnier

BEAUTIFUL
Snifter, No Ice
  3/4 oz Cognac
  3/4 oz Grand Marnier

BEETLE BAILEY
Shake and Strain
  1 1/4 oz B&B
  3/4 oz Bailey's
  Irish Cream

BEND ME OVER EASY
Shake and Strain
  1 oz Amaretto
  3/4 oz Pineapple Juice
  1/4 oz Sour Mix

BETWEEN THE SHEETS
Shake and Strain
  3/4 oz Brandy
  3/4 oz Rum
  3/4 oz Triple Sec
  Splash Sour Mix

BIG BAMBOO
Shake and Strain
  3/4 oz Light Rum
  3/4 oz Myers's Dark Rum
  3/4 oz Tia Maria
  Splash Pina Colada Mix

BIG F___
Shake and Strain
  1 oz Bacardi 151°
  1/4 oz Sambuca
  1/4 oz Peppermint
  Schnapps

BIG FAT ONE PLEASE!
Shake and Strain
  3/4 oz Vodka
  3/4 oz Cointreau
  3/4 oz Midori

BIKINI LINE
  Tia Maria
  Chambord
  Vodka
  Flaming not recommended

BIT O HONEY I
  W. Creme de Cacao
  Bailey's Irish Cream

BIT O HONEY II
Shake and Strain
  1/2 oz Buttershots
  1/2 oz Kahlua
  1/2 oz Bailey's
  Irish Cream
  1/2 oz Frangelico
  1/2 oz Cream

BITTER SCOT
Shake and Strain
  1 1/4 oz Scotch
  3/4 oz Sour Mix
  Splash Rose's
  Lime Juice

B JOB
Layer
  Grand Marnier
  Bailey's Irish Cream
  Whipped Cream

BJ SHOOTER
Layer
  Bailey's Irish Cream
  Irish Whiskey

BLACK AND BLUE
Shake and Strain
  1 oz Blueberry Schnapps
  1 oz Blackberry Schnapps
  Dash Orange Juice
  Dash Cranberry Juice

BLACK APACHE
Shake and Strain
  1 1/4 oz Yukon Jack
  3/4 oz Amaretto
  Splash Sour Mix

BLACK BIRD
Shake and Strain
  1 1/4 oz Blended Whiskey
  3/4 oz Sloe Gin

BLACK CAT
  Kahlua
  Apricot Brandy
  Ouzo

BLACK JACK
  Kahlua
  Anisette

BLACK MASS
  Kahlua
  Sambuca
  151° Rum
  Flaming not recommended

BLACK OUT
Shake and Strain
  1 1/4 oz Gin
  3/4 oz Blackberry Liqueur
  Splash Rose's Lime Juice

BLACK WIDOW
Shake and Strain
  1 1/4 oz Rum
  3/4 oz Kahlua

"Simply SHOOTERS"

B

BLADE RUNNER
Irish Cream
Peppermint Schnapps

BLEEDING BRAIN
Swirl, Rocks Glass
1 1/4 oz Bailey's
Irish Cream
Add Drops of Grenadine

BLOOD CLOT SHOOTER
1 1/4 oz Bacardi
151° Rum
Top with Grenadine
Float Cream on Top

BLOODY BRAIN
Bailey's Irish Cream
Peach Schnapps
2 or 3 Drops Grenadine

BLOODY RUSSIAN
Layer
Stolichnaya Pertsovka
Bloody Mary Mix
Lime Garnish

BLOW J__ I
Kahlua
Bailey's Irish Cream
Whipped Cream

BLOW J__ II
Kahlua
Amaretto
Whipped Cream

BLOW J__ III
Shake and Strain
3/4 oz Banana Liqueur
3/4 oz Grand Marnier
3/4 oz Tia Maria

BLOW SLOW
Layer
Creme de Banana
Irish Cream
Whipped Cream
Drink Using No Hands...

BLUE BERRY TEA
Shake and Strain
1/2 Grand Marnier
1/2 Amaretto
3/4 Ice Tea

BLUE FLAME I
Layer
Galliano
Bacardi 151° Rum
Flaming not recommended

BLUE FLAME II
Southern Comfort
Drambuie
Flaming not recommended

BLUE ICE
Shake and Strain
1 1/4 Peppermint
Schnapps
3/4 oz Blue Curacao
Splash of Cream

BLUE KAMIKAZE
Shake and Strain
  1/2 oz Vodka
  1/2 oz Blue Curacao
  1/2 oz Rose's Lime Juice

BLUE MOON CAFE
  Blue Curacao
  Orange Juice
  Top with Champagne

BLUE POPPER
Shake and Strain
  1 1/4 oz Tequila
  3/4 oz Blue Curacao

BLUE STEEL
Shake and Strain
  1 1/4 oz Vodka
  3/4 oz Peppermint
  Schnapps
  1/2 oz Blue Curacao

BLUE VALIUM
Shake and Strain
  1/2 oz Vodka
  1/2 oz Blue Curacao
  1/2 oz Bailey's
  Irish Cream
  1/2 oz Frangelico

BLUE WHALE I
Shake and Strain
  1/2 oz Vodka
  1/2 oz Rum
  1/2 oz Gin
  1/2 oz Blue Curacao
  Splash 7-Up

BLUE WHALE II
Shake and Strain
  1 oz Rum
  1/2 oz Blue Curacao
  1/2 oz Pineapple Juice

BLUSHIN' RUSSIAN
Shake and Strain
  1 1/4 oz Vodka
  3/4 oz Kahlua
  Splash Cream

BOB MARLEY
Layer
  1/2 Peppermint Schnapps
  1/2 Myers's Dark Rum

BOCCI BALL
Shake and Strain
  1 1/4 oz Vodka
  1/2 oz Amaretto
  Splash Orange Juice

BOILER MAKER
  1 1/4 oz Whiskey
  Drop Shot Into
  Mug of Beer

BOLSHOI PUNCH
Shake and Strain
  1 1/4 oz Vodka
  One Barspoon Sugar
  1/4 oz Rum
  Splash Creme de Cassis

BOMBER
Shake and Strain
  3/4 oz Amaretto
  3/4 oz Vodka
  3/4 oz Pineapple Juice

BON BON
Shake and Strain
  Chambord
  Bailey's Irish Cream
  Truffles Chocolat

BONZAI
Shake and Strain
  1 oz Gin
  1/2 oz Triple Sec
  1/2 oz Roses's Lime Juice

BOSS
Shake and Strain
  1 1/4 oz Bourbon
  3/4 oz Amaretto

BOTTOM BOUNCER
Layer
  Bailey's Irish Cream
  Butterscotch Schnapps

BOURBON STREET
Layer
  Amaretto
  Bourbon

BRAIN HEMORRHAGE
Layer
  Bailey's Irish Cream
  Grenadine
  151° Rum
  Flaming not recommended

BRAIN SHOOTER I
Layer
  Peppermint Schnapps
  Bailey's Irish Cream
  Add Drops Grenadine

BRAIN SHOOTER II
Layer
  Strawberry Liqueur
  Bailey's Irish Cream
  (Drop By Drop)
  Add Drops Grenadine

BRAIN STARTER
Layer
  Kahlua
  Grand Marnier
  Vodka
  Flaming not recommended

BRAIN TUMOR
  Peach Schnapps
  Bailey's Irish Cream
  Grenadine

BRAIN WAVE
Layer
  Bailey's Irish Cream
  Vodka
  2 Drops Grenadine

BRAINS
Layer
  Apple Schnapps
  Bailey's Irish Cream
  (Drop By Drop)

BRAINTEASER
Layer
  Amaretto
  Sloe Gin
  2 Drops Bailey's
  Irish Cream

BRASS BULLETT
Layer
  Benedictine
  Jack Daniels
  Flaming not recommended

BRAVE BULL
Layer
  Kahlua
  Tequila
  Flaming not recommended

BRIDES TEARS OF JOY
Stir and Strain
  1 oz Vodka
  1 oz Silver Aqua D'Ora or
  Silver Wasser

BRONX
Shake and Strain
  1 oz Gin
  1/2 oz S. Vermouth
  1/2 oz D. Vermouth
  Splash Orange Juice

BUBBLEGUM
Shake and Strain
  1/2 oz Vodka
  1/2 oz Banana Liqueur
  1/2 oz Midori
  1/2 oz Orange Juice
  Splash Grenadine

BUBBLEGUM SMASH
Shake and Strain
  1 1/2 oz Rum
  1/2 oz Triple Sec
  1 oz Sour Mix
  Splash Soda
  Splash Grenadine
  2 Dashes Bitters

BUCKING BRONCO
Layer
  Southern Comfort
  Tequila

BUCKINGHAM PALACE
Shake and Strain
  1 1/4 Amaretto di Sarrona
  3/4 oz Crown Royal
  Whisky
  Splash Cranberry Juice

BUFFALO BLOOD
Blackberry Brandy
Bourbon

BUFFALO SWEAT
Rocks Glass, No Ice
1 1/2 oz Bourbon
Dash Tabasco Sauce

BUGER IN THE GRASS
Rocks Glass, Over Ice
1 1/2 oz Midori
1/2 oz Bailey's Irish Cream

BULLFIGHTER
Kahlua
Tequila

BUMBLE BEE
Shake and Strain
1 oz Southern Comfort
1 oz Jack Daniels

BUSHWHACKED
Shake and Strain
1/4 oz W. Creme de Cacao
1/4 oz Cream of Coconut
1/4 oz Kahlua
1/4 oz Bacardi 151°
Splash Cream

BUSTED CHERRY
Kahlua
Cherry Liqueur
Cream

BUSTED RUBBERS
Layer
Raspberry Liqueur
Bailey's Irish Cream
Orange Curacao

BUTTER BABY
Layer
Bailey's Irish Cream
Butterscotch

BUTTERBALL
Shake and Strain
1 oz Butterscotch
1/2 oz Grand Marnier

BUTTERFINGER
Layer
Truffle's Chocolate
Butterscotch
Bailey's Irish Cream

BVD
Stir and Strain
1/2 oz Gin
1/2 oz Rum
1/2 oz D. Vermouth

BY THE POOL
Shake and Strain
3/4 oz Midori
3/4 oz Peach Schnapps
Orange Juice
Top with 7-Up

C&B
Snifter Glass
  Cognac
  Benedictine

CALIFORNIA CRUSH
Shake and Strain
  1 1/4 oz Vodka
  3/4 oz Triple Sec
  Splash Pineapple Juice
  Splash Sour Mix

CALIFORNIA ROOT BEER
Shake and Strain
  1 1/4 oz Kahlua
  3/4 oz Galliano
  Splash Soda Water

CAMEL'S HUMP
  Kahlua
  Apricot Brandy
  Creme de Grand Marnier

CANDY APPLE
Layer
Spoon Float
  1 1/4 oz Apple Schnapps
  3/4 oz Cherry Brandy

CANDY ASSO
Layer
  Chambord
  D. Creme de Cacao

CANDY CANE
  W. Creme de Cacao
  Peppermint Schnapps

CANYON SLIDER
  Peppermint Schnapps
  Bourbon

CAPTAIN COOK
Shake and Strain
  1 1/4 oz Rum
  3/4 oz Grand Marnier
  Splash Pineapple Juice

CARIBBEAN CRUISE
Shake and Strain
  1/2 oz Myers's Rum Cream
  1/2 oz Kahlua
  1/2 oz Vodka
  Splash Cream

CARIBBEAN QUEEN
Shake and Strain
  1/4 oz Malibu Rum
  1/4 oz Myers's Dark Rum
  1/4 oz Mount Gay Rum
  1/4 oz Bacardi Rum
  1/4 oz Amaretto
  Splash Orange Juice
  Splash Pineapple Juice

CARIBBEAN SUNSET
Layer
  Kahlua
  Chambord
  Tia Maria

CARTEL BUSTER
Layer
Tia Maria
Grand Marnier
Tequila

CARTEL SHOOTER
Chambord
Vodka
Grapefruit Juice
Sweet and Sour

CARTEL'S BITE
Cointreau
Cognac
Flaming not recommended

CASPER THE GHOST
Anisette
Tequila

CAT-ASTROPHE
Blend and Strain
1/2 oz Amaretto
1/2 oz Kahlua
1/2 oz Grand Marnier
Splash Coconut Syrup
Splash Cream

CATCH 22
Drambuie
Cointreau

CC RIDER
Chambord
Champagne

CEREBRAL HEMMORHAGE
Layer
Strawberry Liqueur
Bailey's Irish Cream
Grenadine

CHAMBORD SHOOTER
Shake and Strain
3/4 oz Vodka
3/4 oz Chambord
1 oz Cranberry Juice

CHAOS
Shake and Strain
3/4 oz Vodka
3/4 oz Amaretto
3/4 Triple Sec
Splash Sour Mix

CHEAP SHADES
Shake and Strain
3/4 oz Midori
3/4 oz Peach Schnapps
Splash Orange Juice
Splash Pineapple Juice
Splash Sour Mix

CHERNOBEL
Layer
Grand Marnier
Vodka
151° Rum
Flaming not recommended

C

CHERRY BEAN
Layer
   Cherry Herring
   Ouzo
   Flaming not recommended

CHERRY BOMBER
   1/2 oz Grenadine
   Top with 1/2 oz Bacardi
   151° Rum
   Flaming not recommended

CHERRY KISS
   Bailey's Irish Cream
   Chambord

CHERRY LIFESAVER
Layer
   Creme de Noyaux
   Cherry Brandy
   Vodka
   Flaming not recommended

CHILCO
Shake and Strain
   1/2 oz Cointreau
   1/2 oz Bacardi 151°
   1/2 oz Wild Turkey 101°
   Splash Orange Juice
   Splash Cranberry Juice
   Splash Sour Mix

CHIMNEY SWEEP
   1 oz Bourbon
   1 oz Grand Marnier
   Dash Powdered Nutmeg

CHIP SHOT
Layer
   Kahlua
   Bailey's Irish Cream
   Half & Half

CHOCO-AMARETTO SOUFFLE
Layer
   D. Creme de Cacao
   Amaretto
   Cream

CHOCOLATE BANANA
Layer
   D. Creme de Cacao
   Creme de Banana

CHOCOLATE BANANA CREAM PIE
Shake and Strain
   3/4 oz D. Creme de Cacao
   3/4 oz Creme de Banana
   Splash Half & Half

CHOCOLATE CHIP
Layer
   Kahlua
   Bailey's Irish Cream
   D. Creme de Cacao

SHOOTERS"

28

C

CHOCOLATE COVERED CHERRY
Shake and Strain
3/4 oz Cherry Brandy
3/4 oz D. Creme de Cacao
3/4 oz Bailey's Irish Cream

CHOCOLATE CREAM PEACHES
Layer
Kahlua
Peach Schnapps
Half & Half

CHOCOLATE KISS
Layer
D. Creme de Cacao
Half and Half

CHOCOLATE RATTLER
Layer
Kahlua
Bailey's Irish Cream
Peppermint

CHOCOLATE RATTLESNAKE
Layer
Kahlua
G. Creme de Menthe
Grand Marnier

CHOCOLATE SHAKE
Shake and Strain
3/4 oz D. Creme de Cacao
3/4 oz Kahlua
Splash Half & Half

CHOCOLATE TURKEY
Shake and Strain
1/2 oz Wild Turkey 101°
1/2 oz Kahlua
1/2 oz Amaretto
1/2 oz Cherry Brandy

CHOCOLATE TURTLE
Shake and Strain
3/4 oz Praline Liqueur
3/4 oz D. Creme de Cacao
Splash Half & Half

CHRISTMAS SEASON
Layer
Creme de Almond
Midori

CHRISTMAS TREE
Layer
Grenadine
W. Creme de Cacao
G. Creme de Menthe

CHUCKIE
Shake and Strain
1 1/4 oz Vodka
3/4 oz Triple Sec
Splash Pineapple Juice

CINNAMON KISS
Shake and Strain
  1 1/2 oz Cinnamon
  Schnapps
  3/4 oz Grenadine

CIRCUS PEANUTS
Shake and Strain
  Banana Liqueur
  Frangelico
  Kahlua
  Cream
  Pineapple Juice

CITRUS SHOOTER
Shake and Strain
  1 1/4 oz Vodka
  3/4 oz Triple Sec
  Splash Pineapple
  Splash Cranberry
  Splash Grapefruit

CLIMAX
Shake and Strain
  1/2 oz Amaretto
  1/2 oz W. Creme de Cacao
  1/2 oz Triple Sec
  1/2 oz Banana Liqueur
  1/2 oz Vodka
  1/2 oz Cream

CLIMAX SHOOTER
Layer
  Kahlua
  Southern Comfort
  Half & Half

CLIMAX TOGETHER
Shake and Strain
  1/2 oz W. Creme de Cacao
  1/2 oz Triple Sec
  1/2 oz Banana Liqueur
  1/2 oz Vodka
  Splash Cream

COCAINE LADY
Shake and Strain
  1/2 oz Vodka
  1/2 oz Kahlua
  1/2 oz Amaretto
  Splash Cream
  Splash Cola

COCAINE SHOOTER
Shake and Strain
  1 oz Vodka
  1 oz Blackberry Liqueur
  Splash Grapefruit Juice

COCONUT MILK
Shake and Strain
  1 oz Rum
  1 oz Coco Lopez
  1 oz 7-Up

COLD TURKEY
Shake and Strain
  1 1/4 oz Wild Turkey
  3/4 oz Peppermint
  Schnapps

C

COLOR ME PURPLE
Shake and Strain
- 1/2 oz Vodka
- 1/2 oz Triple Sec
- 1/2 oz Peach Schnapps
- 1/2 oz Apple Schnapps
- Splash Grape Juice
- Splash Pineapple Juice

COMA
Layer
- Kahlua
- Anisette
- Grand Marnier

COMMUNIST
Layer
- Kummel
- Vodka
Flaming not recommended

COMMUTER SHOOTER
Shake and Strain
- 1 oz Vodka
- 1/2 oz Triple Sec
- 1/2 oz Amaretto
- 1/2 oz Rose's
- Lime Juice

CON MUSCO
Cordial Glass
- 1 1/2 oz Sambuca
- 3 Coffee Beans

CONCORDE
Layer
- Kahlua
- Bailey's Irish Cream
- Bacardi 151°
Flaming not recommended

CONFETTI
Shake and Strain
- 1 1/4 oz Bailey's Irish Cream
- 3/4 oz Frangelico
- Splash Cream

CONFUSION
Shake and Strain
- 1/2 oz Apple Schnapps
- Splash Creme de Cassis
- Splash Cranberry Juice

CONTINENTAL
- W. Creme de Menthe
- Galliano
- Metaxa

COOKIE
- Kahlua
- W. Creme de Menthe
- Bailey's Irish Cream

COOKIES AND CREAM
Layer
- Kahlua
- W. Creme de Cacao
- Cream

COOL-AIDE
Layer
  Midori
  Cranberry Juice

COOL CAPTAIN
Layer
  Grenadine
  Peppermint Schnapps
  Captain Morgan's Rum

COON DOG
Shake and Strain
  3/4 oz Jack Daniels
  3/4 oz Blackberry Liqueur
  Splash Sour Mix

CORKSCREW
Shake and Strain
  1 1/4 oz Rum
  3/4 oz Peach Schnapps
  Splash Dry Vermouth
  Splash 7-Up
  Splash Orange Juice

CORTISONE
Shake and Strain
  3/4 oz Tia Maria
  3/4 oz W. Creme de Cacao
  3/4 oz Rum

COSMOPOLITAN
Shake and Strain
  1 1/4 oz Vodka
  3/4 oz Triple Sec
  Splash Apple Schnapps
  Splash Cranberry Juice
  Splash Rose's
  Lime Juice

COUGH DROP
Shake and Strain
  Blackberry Brandy
  Peppermint Schnapps

COUNTDOWN BEGINS
Shake and Strain
  1 1/2 oz Cointreau
  1/2 oz Rose's
  Lime Juice

COW CATCHER
Do Not Chill
  1 1/4 oz Tequila
  3/4 oz Kahlua

CRANBERRY SHOOTER
Shake and Strain
  1 1/2 oz Vodka
  1 oz Cranberry Juice
  1/2 oz Sour Mix

C

CRANBERRY SMASH
Shake and Strain
 1 oz Vodka
 1 oz Apple Schnapps
 Splash Cranberry Juice
 Squeeze Lime

CREAM OF BEEF
Shake and Strain
 1 1/4 oz Bailey's
 Irish Cream
 3/4 oz Beefeater Gin

CREAMSICLE
Shake and Strain
 1 1/4 oz Amaretto
 3/4 oz Triple Sec
 Splash Orange Juice

CREME DE LA CREME
Shake and Strain
 3/4 oz Brandy
 3/4 oz Tia Maria
 3/4 D. Creme de Cacao
 Splash Cream

CRISPY
Shake and Strain
 1 1/4 oz Kahlua
 3/4 oz Amaretto
 3/4 oz Peppermint
 Schnapps

CROWLEY'S CREAMER
Shake and Strain
 1 oz Amaretto
 1/2 oz D. Creme de
 Cacao
 Splash Half & Half

CYRANO
Shake and Strain
 1 oz Bailey's
 Irish Cream
 1 oz Grand Marnier
 1/2 oz Chambord

DC-10 I
Kahlua
Bailey's Irish Cream
Amaretto

DC-10 II
Shake and Strain
3/4 oz Vodka
3/4 oz D. Creme de
Cacao
3/4 oz Amaretto
Whipped Cream

DALLAS ALICE
Tia Maria
Grand Marnier
Tequila Gold

DEAD RAT SHOOTER
Shake and Strain
1 1/4 oz Scotch
3/4 Green Chartreuse

DEAD TEDDY
Layer
Bailey's Irish Cream
Midori
Cointreau

DEATHWISH
Layer
Grenadine
Peppermint Schnapps
Wild Turkey Liqueur
151° Rum
Flaming not recommended

DEEP THROAT I
Kahlua
Bailey's Irish Cream
Vodka

DEEP THROAT II
Kahlua
Bailey's Irish Cream
Vodka
Whipped Cream

DEEP THROAT III
Pony Glass
Kahlua or Tia Maria
Vodka
Whipped Cream
Drink With No Hands

DEFROSTER
Yukon Jack
Bourbon
Flaming not recommended

DENNIS THE MENACE
Shake and Strain
Equal Parts:
Peach Schnapps, Malibu
Orange Juice
Cranberry Juice

DEPTH CHARGE
1/2 Glass of Beer
1 Shot Glass of
Peppermint Schnapps
Drop Shot Into Beer

DESIGNER JEANS

Shake and Strain
3/4 oz Bailey's Irish Cream
3/4 oz Raspberry Schnapps
3/4 oz Myers's Dark Rum

DEVINE WIND

Shake and Strain
1 oz Vodka
1/2 oz Blue Curacao
1/2 oz Rose's
Lime Juice

DIAMOND JIM

Shake and Stain
1 oz Rum
1/2 oz Amaretto
Equal Splash Juice of
Orange, Cranberry,
Pineapple, Sour Mix

DIANA

Layer
W. Creme de Menthe
Brandy
Flaming not recommended

DIRT

Shake and Strain
3/4 oz Vodka
3/4 oz Kahlua
1/4 oz Galliano
Float 1/2 oz 151° Rum
Flaming not recommended

DIRTY ASHTRAY

Layer
Kahlua
G. Creme de Menthe
Flaming not recommended

DIRTY BANANA

Shake and Strain
3/4 oz Banana Liqueur
3/4 oz Kahlua
3/4 oz Cream

DIRTY HARRY

Layer
Tia Maria
Grand Marnier

DIRTY MONKEY

Layer
Banana Liqueur
Kahlua
Bailey's Irish Cream

DIRTY MOUSE

Shake and Strain
3/4 oz Vodka
3/4 oz Kahlua
3/4 oz Bailey's
Irish Cream
3/4 oz Frangelico

DOA

Anisette
Parfait Amour
Tequila

DOLLAR BILLY
1 oz Vodka
1/2 oz Midori
1/2 oz Sour Mix

DOLLAR SHOT
Each person takes a dollar bill, using the first three numbers, count from top left and use the corresponding bottles.
Pour:
1/2 oz of Each Into
Shot Glass

DOUBLE JACKASS
Layer
Yukon Jack
Jack Daniels

DOUBLEMINT
Peppermint Schnapps
Spearmint Schnapps

DOWNHILL RACER
Shake and Strain
3/4 oz Bacardi
151° Rum
3/4 oz Amaretto
3/4 oz Pineapple Juice

DR. COLA
Shake and Strain
1 1/2 oz Vodka
1/2 oz Amaretto
Top with Cola

DR. PEPPER I
1 1/2 oz Amaretto
Fill with Soda

DR. PEPPER II
In a Shot Glass
3/4 oz Amaretto
1/2 oz Rum
Flame;
Drop Into Mug of Beer
Flaming not recommended

DRAGOON
Kahlua
Bailey's Irish Cream
Sambuca
Flaming not recommended

DUCK FART
Kahlua
Bailey's Irish Cream
Crown Royal
Flaming not recommended

DUSTY ROSE
Chambord
Bailey's Irish Cream

DYNAMIC DUO
Shake and Strain
1/2 oz Vodka
1/2 oz D. Creme de Cacao
1/2 oz Grand Marnier
Splash Orange Juice

E.T. I

Peppermint Schnapps
Tequila
151° Rum
Flaming not recommended

E.T. II

Midori
Bailey Irish Cream
Vodka
Flaming not recommended

EARTHQUAKE

Anisette
Amaretto
Southern Comfort

EASTER EGG HUNT

Layer
Kahlua
Raspberry Schnapps
Cream

ECLIPSE

Blackberry Brandy
Golden Tequila
Flaming not recommended

ECSTACY SHOOTER

Shake and Strain
3/4 oz Raspberry
Schnapps
3/4 oz Vodka
Splash Orange Juice,
Cranberry Juice

ED COLLINS

Anisette
Peppermint Schnapps

EL CHICO

Shake and Strain
1 oz Tequila
1/2 oz Triple Sec
1/2 oz Rose's Lime
Juice
Dash of Angostura Bitters

ELECTRIC BANANA

Shake and Strain
3/4 oz Rum
3/4 oz Banana Liqueur
3/4 oz Sour Mix

ELECTRIC CHAIR

Drambuie
Peppermint Schnapps
Grand Marnier

ELECTRIC CHERRY COLA

Shake and Strain
1 1/4 oz Crown Royal
3/4 Cherry Brandy
Splash Cola

ELECTRIC ICE TEA

Shake and Strain
Vodka, Rum, Gin
Triple Sec, Tequila
Sour Mix
Top with 7-Up

ELECTRIC KOOLAIDE
Shake and Strain
Equal Parts:
Southern Comfort,
Amaretto, Triple Sec,
Midori, Cherry Liqueur,
Sour Mix, Cranberry
Dash of Grenadine

ELEPHANT WIND BREAKER (FART)
Layer
Jack Daniels
Bacardi 151° Rum
Flaming not recommended

EMBOLISM
Chambord
Bailey's Irish Cream

EMERALD
1 1/4 oz Brandy
3/4 oz G. Creme de Menthe

EMPIRE SLAMMER
Shake and Strain
1/2 oz Canadian Whisky
1/2 oz Creme de Banana
1/2 oz Sloe Gin
1/2 oz Orange Juice

EMPTY THE SHOOTER (ETS)
Creme de Banana
Malibu
Dark Rum
Flaming not recommended

ER...ECTION
Layer
G. Creme de Menthe
Champagne

ETHEL DUFFY
Shake and Strain
3/4 oz Apricot Brandy
3/4 oz W. Creme de Menthe
3/4 oz Orange Curacao

EUROPEAN BEAUTY
Snifter Glass
1/2 Cognac
1/2 Amaretto

EVE
Shake and Strain
3/4 oz Vodka
3/4 oz Apple Schnapps
Splash Orange Juice
Splash Pineapple Juice

EVERGLADES
Layer
W. Creme de Cacao
Cream
Rum
Dash Kahlua

EYE TO EYE
Shake and Strain
3/4 oz Irish Whiskey
3/4 oz Bailey's Irish Cream

F

F-16
Layer
Kahlua
Bailey's Irish Cream
Frangelico

F-52
Shake and Strain
1/2 oz Kahlua or Tia Maria
1/2 oz Bailey's Irish Cream
1/2 oz Frangelico

FAHRENHEIT 5000
Rocks Glass, No Ice
1 oz Cinnamon
Schnapps
1 oz Absolut Vodka
Peppar

FERRARI
Layer
Amaretto
Cream

FIDCORP
Shake and Strain
1 oz Vodka
1/2 oz Amaretto
1/2 oz Peach Brandy
1/2 oz Sour Mix

FIFTH AVENUE I
Shake and Strain
1/2 oz Bailey's Irish Cream
1/2 oz Apricot Brandy
1/2 oz W. Creme de Cacao

FIFTH AVENUE II
Layer
D. Creme de Cacao
Apricot Brandy
Cream

FINE TONER
Shake and Strain
1 1/4 oz Stolichnaya
3/4 oz Peach Brandy

'57 CHEVY
Shake and Strain
1/2 oz Rum
1/2 oz Amaretto
1/2 oz Banana Liqueur
1/2 oz Southern Comfort
Splash Orange Juice,
Pineapple Juice
Dash Grenadine

'57 CHEVY WITH CALIFORNIA PLATES
Shake and Strain
1/2 oz Rum
1/2 oz Amaretto
1/2 oz Southern Comfort
1/2 oz Creme de Almond
Splash Orange Juice

'57 CHEVY WITH FLORIDA PLATES

Shake and Strain
 1/2 oz Dark Rum
 1/2 oz Amaretto
 1/2 oz Southern Comfort
 1/2 Creme de Almond
 Splash Orange Juice,
 Grapefruit Juice

'57 CHEVY WITH HAWAIIAN PLATES

Shake and Strain
 1/2 oz Dark Rum
 1/2 oz Amaretto
 1/2 oz Southern Comfort
 1/2 oz Creme de Almond
 Splash Pineapple Juice

'57 CHEVY WITH TOP DOWN

Shake and Strain
 1/2 oz Grand Marnier
 1/2 oz Amaretto
 1/2 oz Southern Comfort
 1/2 oz Creme de Almond
 Splash Pineapple Juice

'57 T-BIRD CONVERTIBLE

Shake and Strain
 3/4 oz Southern Comfort
 3/4 oz Grand Marnier
 (Optional)
 3/4 oz Amaretto
 Splash Pineapple Juice

FIRE AND ICE

Layer
 Peppermint Schnapps
 Bacardi 151° Rum
 Flaming not recommended

FIRE IN THE HOLE

Layer
 Ouzo
 2 or 3 Drops Tabasco

FIRE STARTER

Layer
 1/2 Brandy
 1/2 Cinnamon Schnapps

FIREBALL SHOOTER I

Layer
 Cinnamon Schnapps
 Cherry Liqueur

FIREBALL SHOOTER II

Layer
 Cinnamon Schnapps
 Dash Tabasco

FIRECRACKER

Shake and Strain
Sugar Rim of Glass
 1 1/4 oz Seagram's 7
 Splash Cranberry Juice

FIREFLY

Layer
 W. Creme de Menthe
 Bacardi 151° Rum

FIREWORKS

Layer
  Grenadine
  Creme de Cassis
  Apricot Brandy
  Cointreau
  Green Chartreuse
  Cognac
  Kirschwasser
  Flaming not recommended

FLAMING ANGEL

  Peppermint Schnapps
  Southern Comfort
  Bacardi 151° Rum
  Flaming not recommended

FLAMING ARMADILLO

Layer
  Kahlua
  Amaretto
  Grand Marnier
  Brandy
  Flaming not recommended

FLAMING DR. PEPPER I

  1 1/2 oz Amaretto
  Fill with Soda

FLAMING DR. PEPPER II

In a Shot Glass
  3/4 oz Amaretto
  1/2 oz Rum
  Flame, Drop Into
  Mug of Beer
  Flaming not recommended

FLAMING GORILLA

Layer
  Kahlua
  Wild Turkey 101°
  Bacardi 151° Rum
  Flaming not recommended

FLAMING HOOKER

Layer
  Galliano
  Cognac
  Bacardi 151° Rum
  Flaming not recommended

FLAMING JELLY BEAN

Layer
  Kahlua
  Cherry Brandy
  Wild Turkey 101°
  Bacardi 151° Rum
  Flaming not recommended

FLAMING ORGASM

Layer
  Kahlua
  Galliano
  Bacardi 151° Rum
  Flaming not recommended

FLAMING SHORTS

Layer
  Kahlua
  Bailey's Irish Cream
  Green Chartreuse
  Flaming not recommended

FLEE BALL
Layer
  Cinnamon Schnapps
  Cherry Brandy

FLIGHT JACKET
Layer
  Kahlua
  Bailey's Irish Cream
  Irish Mist

FLOATER
  1 1/4 oz Crown Royal
  3/4 oz Peppermint
  Schnapps

FLORIDA BAY SHOOTER
Shake and Strain
  1 1/2 oz Vodka
  1/2 oz Cointreau
  Dash Grenadine
  Splash Orange Juice

FLYING ARMADILLO
Layer
  3/4 oz Amaretto
  1/4 151° Rum

FLYING F___
Layer
  Frangelico
  Vodka
  Flaming not recommended

FLYING GRASSHOPPER
Shake and Strain
  3/4 oz G. Creme de Menthe
  3/4 oz W. Creme de Cacao
  3/4 oz Vodka

FLYING TIGER
Shake and Strain
  3/4 oz Galliano
  3/4 oz W. Creme de Menthe
  3/4 oz Vodka

FOG
Shake and Strain
  1 1/4 oz Vodka
  Splash Cranberry Juice
  Dash Rose's Lime Juice

FOUR BY FOUR (4 X 4)
Shake and Strain
  1/4 oz Gin
  1/4 oz Rum
  1/4 oz Tequila
  1/4 oz Amaretto
  1/4 oz Triple Sec
  1/4 oz Creme de Cacao
  1/4 oz Apricot Liqueur

FOUR LEAF CLOVER
Shake and Strain
1/2 oz Gin
1/2 oz Vodka
1/2 oz Triple Sec
1/2 oz Blue Curacao
Splash 7-Up, Sour Mix

FOURTH OF JULY
Layer
Grenadine
W. Creme de Menthe
Blue Curacao

FOXY LADY
Shake and Strain
3/4 oz Vodka
3/4 oz Kahlua
3/4 oz Amaretto
Splash Cream

FREDDY KRUGER
Layer
Ouzo
Jagermeister
Vodka

FREEBASE
Shake and Strain
1/2 oz Kahlua
1/2 oz Rum
1/2 oz Myers's Rum Cream
Top with Bacardi 151° Rum
Suck Through a Straw

FRENCH CONNECTION
Shake and Strain
1 1/4 oz Cognac
3/4 oz Amaretto

FRENCH KISS BEST!
Shake and Strain
1 1/4 oz Smirnoff Vodka
1/4 oz Grand Marnier
1/4 oz Cointreau
1/4 oz Chambord
Splash Cranberry Juice

FRUIT LOOP I
Shake and Strain
3/4 oz Banana Liqueur
3/4 oz Midori
3/4 Strawberry Liqueur

FRUIT LOOP II
Shake and Strain
3/4 oz Apple Schnapps
3/4 oz Cherry Liqueur
3/4 oz Vodka
Splash Orange Juice

F

F___ IT!!
Shake and Strain
  1/2 oz Frangelico
  1/2 oz D. Creme de
  Cacao
  1/2 oz Bailey's
  Irish Cream
  1/2 oz Tia Maria
  1/2 oz Vodka
  Splash Cream

FULL MOON
Snifter, No Ice
  3/4 oz Grand Marnier
  3/4 oz Amaretto

FUNKY MONKEY
Shake and Strain
  3/4 oz Rum
  3/4 oz Banana Liqueur
  Splash Orange Juice

FUTURE SHOOTER
Layer
  Cognac
  Kahlua
  Cola

FUZZ BALL
Shake and Strain
  1 oz Vodka
  1/2 oz Peach Schnapps
  1 oz Orange Juice

FUZZY BELLY BUTTON
Shake and Strain
  1 1/4 oz Peach
  Schnapps
  3/4 oz Triple Sec
  Splash Orange Juice

FUZZY BUSH
Layer
  Old Bushmills Irish
  Whiskey
  Peach Schnapps

FUZZY MOTHER I
Layer
  Tequila
  Amaretto
  Bacardi 151° Rum
  Flaming not recommended

FUZZY MOTHER II
Layer
  Amaretto
  Galliano

G - SPOT
Shake and Strain
3/4 oz Stolichnaya
3/4 oz Grand Marnier
3/4 oz Cranberry Juice

GALLIGHER'S FLOAT
Shake and Strain
1 1/4 oz Galliano
3/4 oz Cream
Top with Cola

GANDY DANCING
Shake and Strain
1/2 oz Creme de Almond
1/2 oz Yukon Jack
1/2 oz Creme de Banana
Splash Pineapple Juice

GEORGIA CREAM
Shake and Strain
3/4 oz Peach Brandy
3/4 oz W. Creme de Cacao
Splash Cream

GEORGIA PEACH
Shake and Strain
1 1/4 oz Peach Schnapps
3/4 oz Southern Comfort

GEORGIA SWEETHEART
Shake and Strain
1/2 oz Peach Brandy
1/2 oz Peppermint
Schnapps
1/2 oz Banana Liqueur
Splash Cream

GEORGIA WATER-MELON IS BEST
Shake and Strain
1 oz Vodka
3/4 oz Cherry Brandy
1/2 oz Grenadine
Splash Sweet and Sour

GERMAN CHOCOLATE CAKE
Kahlua
Bailey's Irish Cream
Frangelico
Cream

GHOSTBUSTER'S REVISITED
Shake and Strain
1/2 oz Vodka
1/2 oz Gin
1/2 oz Amaretto
1/2 oz Triple Sec
1/2 oz B&B
Splash Cream

G

GIRL SCOUT COOKIE

Shake and Strain
  3/4 oz D. Creme
  de Cacao
  3/4 oz W.Creme
   de Menthe
  Splash Bailey's

GIZMO

Shake and Strain
  3/4 oz Tequila Gold
  3/4 oz Amaretto
  Splash 7-Up

GLAMORAMA

Shake and Strain
  1 1/4 oz Vodka
  3/4 oz Peach Schnapps
  Splash Each: Cranberry,
  Pineapple Juice,
  Sour Mix

GOAL POST

Layer
  Peppermint Schnapps
  Tequila

GOLD NUGGET

Shake and Strain
  1 1/4 Gold Schnapps or
  Galliano
  3/4 oz Amaretto

GOLD RUSH I

Shake and Strain
  1 1/2 oz Cuervo
  Tequila Gold
  1/2 oz Grand Marnier
  1/2 oz Rose's
  Lime Juice

GOLD RUSH II

  Southern Comfort
  Jack Daniels
  Flaming not recommended

GOLDEN APPLE

Shake and Strain
  1 oz Galliano
  3/4 oz Apple Brandy
  3/4 oz W. Creme de Cacao

GOLDEN CREAM

Shake and Strain
  1 1/4 oz Bailey's Irish Cream
  3/4 oz Galliano
  1/2 oz Grand Marnier

GOLDEN GLOW

Shake and Strain
  3/4 oz Galliano
  3/4 oz Drambuie
  3/4 oz Gin

GOLDEN GOPHER

Shake and Strain
  1 1/4 oz W. Creme de
  Cacao
  3/4 oz Brandy

GOLDEN LIRAS
Layer
  Galliano
  Creme de Banana

GOLDEN PEACH
Shake and Strain
  1 1/4 oz Peach Schnapps
  3/4 oz Gin
  1/2 oz Galliano
  Splash Orange Juice

GOLDEN POOFER
Shake and Strain
  1/2 oz W. Creme de Cacao
  1/2 oz Amaretto
  1/2 oz Kahlua
  1/2 oz Frangelico
  1/2 oz Bailey's Irish Cream
  Splash Cream

GOLDEN SIN
Layer
  Cinnamon Schnapps
  Tequila Gold

GOLDEN SLIPPER
Shake and Strain
  1 1/4 oz Vodka
  3/4 oz Galliano
  Splash Orange Juice

GOLDEN SPIKE
Layer
  Galliano
  Drambuie
  Scotch

GOOD AND PLENTY
Layer
  Kahlua
  Pernod

GOOSE JUICE
Layer
  Apricot Brandy
  151° Bacardi Rum
  Flaming not recommended

GORGEOUS
Snifter, No Ice
  3/4 oz Amaretto
  3/4 oz Grand Marnier

GORILLA FART SHOOTER
Shake and Strain
  3/4 oz Bacardi 151° Rum
  3/4 oz Wild Turkey 101°

GORILLA WIND
Layer
  Wild Turkey
  151° Rum
  Flaming not recommended

GOUMBE' SMASH
Shake and Strain
1 1/4 oz Rum
3/4 oz Myers's
Rum Cream
Dash Grenadine
Splash Each: Orange,
Pineapple Juice

GRAND AM
Amaretto
Grand Marnier

GRAND DON
Amaretto
Grand Marnier

GRANDE ALLIANCE
Layer
Amaretto
Champagne

GRANDE RUSH
Shake and Strain
3/4 oz Brandy
3/4 oz Vodka
3/4 oz Chambord
Splash Sour Mix

GREEK REVOLUTION
Layer
Grenadine
Ouzo (Anisette)
Galliano
Vodka
Flaming not recommended

GREEK STINGER
1 1/4 oz Metaxa
3/4 oz Galliano

GREEK TRAGEDY
Layer
Sambuca
Galliano
Ouzo

GREEN APPLE
Layer
Midori
Apple Schnapps

GREEN DAVID
Shake and Strain
1 1/4 oz Gin
3/4 oz G. Creme de
Menthe
Dash Rose's Lime Juice

GREEN DRAGON
Layer
Green Chartreuse
Bacardi 151° Rum
Flaming not recommended

GREEN GENIE
Shake and Strain
1 1/4 oz Vodka
3/4 oz Green Chartreuse

GREEN LIZARD

Shake and Strain
1 1/4 oz Banana Liqueur
1/2 oz Blue Curacao
Splash Orange Juice

GREEN RUSSIAN

Shake and Strain
1 1/4 oz Vodka
3/4 oz Midori

GREEN SNEAKER

Shake and Strain
1 oz Vodka
1/2 oz Melon Liqueur
1/2 oz Cointreau
Splash Cream
Orange Juice

GREEN WEENIE

Layer
Peppermint Schnapps
Midori

GREMLIN

Shake and Strain
1 oz Vodka
1/2 oz Bacardi
Light Rum
1/2 oz Blue Curacao
Splash Orange Juice

GRENADE (HAND)

Layer
Peach Liqueur
Club Soda
Bacardi 151° Rum
Flaming not recommended

GRENADE (RIFLE)

Layer, Rocks Glass
No Ice
1/2 oz Vodka
1/2 oz Rum
1/2 oz Grenadine
Splash 7-Up

GROOM'S TEARS OF JOY

Layer
Goldwasser
W. Creme de Menthe

GUILLOTINE

Shake and Strain
1 oz Vodka
1/2 oz Tequila
1/2 oz W. Creme de
Menthe

GULLET PLEASER

Shake and Strain
1 oz Vodka
1/2 oz Peach Liqueur
Splash of Each: Sour
Mix, Cranberry and
Grapefruit Juice

G

GUM DROP
Shake and Strain
   3/4 oz Scotch
   3/4 oz Galliano

GUMBA
Layer
   Cream of Coconut
   Banana Liqueur
   Tia Maria

HAIRY NAVEL
Shake and Strain
1 1/4 oz Vodka
3/4 oz Peach Schnapps
Orange Juice

HAIRY NUT
Layer
Bailey's Irish Cream
Frangelico

HALF GRAM SHOOTER
Shake and Strain
3/4 oz Grand Marnier
3/4 oz Creme de
Grand Marnier
Cream

HALF MOON
Shake and Strain
1 1/4 oz Grand Marnier
3/4 oz Amaretto

HALLEY'S COMET
Shake and Strain
1 1/4 oz Southern
Comfort
3/4 oz Peach Schnapps
Top with Club Soda

HAND GRENADE
Layer
Jagermeister
Rumple Minze
151° Rum
Flaming not recommended

HAPPY JACK
Rocks Glass, Over Ice
1 1/2 oz Jack Daniels
1/2 oz Applejack
(Schnapps)

HARBOR LIGHT I
Layer
Metaxa
Galliano
Creme de Noyaux

HARBOR LIGHT II
Layer
Kahlua
Tequila
Rum 151°
Flaming not recommended

HARBOR LIGHT III
Layer
Amaretto
Southern Comfort
Galliano

HARBOR LIGHT IV
Layer
Amaretto
Kahlua
Tequila
Brandy
Flaming not recommended

HARBOR LIGHTS
Layer
  Kahlua
  Tequila
  Rum 151°
  Flaming not recommended

HARD DICKSON
Rocks Glass, On Ice
  1 1/4 oz Vodka
  3/4 oz Frangelico
  Splash 7-Up

HASTA LA VISTA, MY BABY
Shake and Strain
  1 1/4 oz Tequila
  Dash Each: Triple Sec,
  Amaretto,
  Peach Schnapps
  Splash Orange,
  Pineapple Juice

HAWAIIAN I
Shake and Strain
  3/4 oz Amaretto
  3/4 oz Vodka
  3/4 oz Cranberry Juice

HAWAIIAN II
Shake and Strain
  Amaretto
  Southern Comfort
  Grenadine
  Splash Orange,
  Pineapple Juice

HAWAIIAN III
Shake and Strain
  1 1/4 oz Vodka
  3/4 oz Cherry Brandy
  Splash Sour Mix
  Dash Grenadine

HAWAIIAN IV
Shake and Strain
  1/2 oz Rum
  1/2 oz Vodka
  1/2 oz Amaretto
  Dash Grenadine
  Splash Orange,
  Pineapple Juice

HAWAIIAN PUNCH
Shake and Strain
  1 1/4 oz Southern
  Comfort
  3/4 oz Creme de Noya
  Splash Orange,
  Pineapple Juice

HAWAIIAN SHOOTER I
Shake and Strain
  1 1/4 oz Southern
  Comfort
  3/4 oz Creme de Noyaux
  Splash Pineapple Juice

HAWAIIAN SHOOTER II

Shake and Strain
- 1/2 oz Rum
- 1/2 oz Vodka
- 1/2 oz Amaretto
- 1/2 oz Grenadine
- Splash Orange Juice

HAWAIIAN SHOOTER III

Shake and Strain
- 3/4 oz Southern Comfort
- 3/4 oz Creme de Almond
- Orange Juice

HAWAIIAN SHOOTER IV

Shake and Strain
- 1/2 oz Amaretto
- 1/2 oz Grand Marnier
- 1/2 oz Southern Comfort
- Splash Pineapple Juice

HEAD INJURY

Shake and Strain
- Vodka
- Peach Schnapps
- Apple Schnapps
- Splash Cranberry Juice
- Top with 7-Up

HEAD ROOM

Layer
- Banana
- Irish Cream
- Midori
- Vodka
- *Flaming not recommended*

HEART ATTACK

Shake and Strain
- 1 oz Cinnamon Schnapps
- 1/2 oz Midori
- 1/2 oz Grenadine

HEARTBURN RELIEF

Shake and Strain
- 1 1/2 oz Cinnamon Schnapps
- 1/2 oz Grenadine
- Drops of Tabasco

HOLLYWOOD

Shake and Strain
- 1 1/4 oz Vodka
- 3/4 oz Chambord
- Splash Cranberry Juice

HONEYBEE

Layer
- Jagermeister
- Barenmeister

HONEYSUCKLE

Shake and Strain
- 1 1/4 oz Rum
- 3/4 oz Simple Syrup
- Splash Sour Mix

HOOCH SHOOTER

Shake and Strain
1/2 oz Vodka
1/2 oz Cherry Brandy
1/2 oz Dark Rum
1/2 oz Midori
Splash Orange,
Cranberry Juice

HOOTER SHOOTER

Shake and Strain
3/4 oz Amaretto
3/4 oz Vodka
1/2 oz Grenadine
Splash Orange Juice

HOP SKIP AND GO NAKED

Shake and Strain
1 1/4 oz Gin
3/4 oz Cherry Brandy
Splash Sour Mix, 7-Up
Splash Draft Beer
Dash Grenadine

HORSESHOE

Shake and Strain
1 1/4 oz Jack Daniels
3/4 oz Peppermint
Schnapps

HOT CHERRY PIE

Rocks Glass, No Ice
1 1/4 Amaretto di
Saronno
Splash Cranberry Juice
(Room Temp)
Float 151° Rum

HOT NUT I

Layer
Frangelico
Tequila
Flaming not recommended

HOT NUT II

Layer
Kahlua
Amaretto
Frangelico
Rum 151°
Flaming not recommended

HOT PANTS

Shake and Strain
Salted Rim
1 1/4 oz Tequila
3/4 oz Peppermint
Schnapps
Splash Grapefruit Juice

HOT SHOTS

Layer
Vodka
Peppermint Schnapps
2 or 3 Drops Tabasco

HOT SUMMER NIGHT

Shake and Strain
   1/2 oz Apple Schnapps
   1/2 oz Peach Schnapps
   1/2 oz 151°
   Splash Cranberry,
   Pineapple Juice

HOT TAMALE

Layer
   Cinnamon Schnapps
   Tequila Gold
   Flaming not recommended

HOT TIMES

Layer
   Apple Schnapps
   Cinnamon Schnapps
   2 or 3 Drops Tabasco
   Vodka
   Flaming not recommended

HUMMER

Shake and Strain
   1 1/4 oz Rum
   3/4 oz Kahlua
   Splash Cream

I TO I
Shake and Strain
   3/4 oz Irish Whiskey
   3/4 oz Bailey's
   Irish Cream

ICE BREAKER
Layer
   Peppermint Schnapps
   Yukon Jack
   Club Soda

ICE BURG
Shake and Strain
   1 1/4 oz Tequila or
   Vodka
   Splash Cranberry
   Juice or Ice Tea

ICE PICK
Shake and Strain
   1 1/4 oz Vodka
   3/4 oz Triple Sec
   Splash Cranberry
   Juice or Ice Tea

ICE TEA SLAMMER
Shake and Strain
Rocks Glass
   Equal Parts: Gin,
   Vodka, Rum,
   Triple Sec
   Splash Sour Mix
   Top with Cola

IGUANA
Shake and Strain
   3/4 oz Vodka
   3/4 Tequila
   3/4 oz Kahlua

IN THE ROUGH
*Any cocktail not
blended but on the
rocks.*

INDIAN SUMMER
Shake and Strain
   1 1/4 oz Vodka
   3/4 Kahlua
   Splash Pineapple
   Juice

INDIANA JONES
Layer
   Blackberry Brandy
   Bacardi 151° Rum
   Flaming not recommended

INNOCENT BYSTANDER
   Frangelico
   Yukon Jack
   Southern Comfort

INSANE HUSSEIN
Shake and Strain
   1 1/4 oz Vodka
   3/4 oz Apple Schnapps
   Splash Grapefruit Juice

I

INSANE TIMES
Layer
  Kahlua
  Blackberry Schnapps

INTERNATIONAL STINGER
Shake and Strain
  1 1/2 oz Metaxa
  1/2 oz Galliano
  1/2 oz W. Creme de
  Menthe (Optional)

IRISH APPLE
Shake and Strain
  1 1/4 oz Apple Schnapps
  3/4 oz Irish Whiskey

IRISH EYE
Shake and Strain
  1 1/4 oz Irish Mist
  3/4 oz Vodka
  Splash Sour Mix, Soda

IRISH FOG
Layer
  Midori Liqueur
  Bailey's Irish Cream

IRISH FROGMAN
Layer
  Melon Liqueur
  Irish Cream
  Irish Whiskey

IRISH FROST
Shake and Strain
  1 1/4 oz Bailey's
  Irish Cream
  3/4 oz Coco Lopez
  Splash Cream

IRISH HEADLOCK
Layer
  Bailey's Irish Cream
  Irish Whiskey
  Amaretto
  Brandy (Cognac)

IRISH MAFIA
Shake and Strain
  1 1/4 oz G. Creme de
  Menthe
  3/4 oz Amaretto
  Splash Cream

IRISH VALIUM
Shake and Strain
  1 1/4 oz Irish Whiskey
  3/4 oz Amaretto

IRON BUTTERFLY
Layer
  Kahlua
  Bailey's Irish Cream
  Vodka

ITALIAN DELIGHT
Shake and Strain
  1 1/4 oz Vodka
  3/4 oz Amaretto
  Orange Juice
  Cream

ITALIAN DOCTOR
Shake and Strain
  1 1/4 oz Amaretto
  3/4 Peppermint
  Schnapps

ITALIAN FLAG
Layer
  Grenadine
  Peppermint Schnapps
  G. Creme de Menthe

ITALIAN STALLION
Shake and Strain
  1 1/4 oz Scotch
  3/4 oz Galliano

ITALIAN VALIUM
Shake and Strain
  1 1/4 oz Gin
  3/4 oz Amaretto

JACK ATTACK
Layer
Peppermint Schnapps
Jack Daniels

JACK 'N THE BEANSTALK
Shake and Strain
1 1/4 oz Jack Daniels
3/4 oz Midori

JACK O
Shake and Strain
1 1/4 oz Jack Daniels
3/4 oz Bailey's
Irish Cream

JAGERSHAKE
Shake and Strain
1/2 oz Jagermeister
1/2 oz Kahlua
1/2 oz D. Creme de Cacao
Splash Cream

JAMAICAN BARBADOS BOMBER
Shake and Strain
3/4 oz Myers's Dark Rum
3/4 oz Mount Gay Rum
1/4 oz Cointreau
1/4 oz Rose's
Lime Juice

JAMAICAN BOBSLED TEAM
Layer
Peppermint Schnapps
Myers's Dark Rum

JAMAICAN DUSTY
Layer
Tia Maria
Myers's Rum Cream
Myers's Dark Rum

JAMAICAN QUAALUDE
Shake and Strain
1 oz Myers's Rum Cream
1 oz Myers's Dark Rum

JAMAICAN RUM CREAM
Shake and Strain
3/4 oz Myers's Dark Rum
3/4 oz Myers's
Rum Cream
3/4 oz Bailey's
Irish Cream
Splash Cream

JAMAICAN TEN SPEED
Layer
Kahlua
Bailey's Irish Cream
Myers's Dark Rum

J

JAWBREAKER (RED HOT)
Layer
  Cinnamon Schnapps
  Grenadine (Optional)
  3 Drops Tabasco

JELLY BEAN I
  Blackberry Liqueur
  Anisette
  Southern Comfort

JELLY BEAN II
Rocks Glass, No Ice
  3/4 oz Blackberry
  Brandy
  3/4 oz Ouzo

JELLY BEAN III
  Grenadine
  Anisette
  Southern Comfort
  Flaming not recommended

JELLY DONUT
  Kahlua
  Chambord
  Bailey's Irish Cream

JELLY FISH I
Layer
  Grenadine
  W. Creme de
  Cacao or Menthe
  Amaretto
  Bailey's Irish Cream

JELLY FISH II
Rocks Glass, No Ice
  1 1/4 oz W. Creme de
  Cacao
  3/4 oz Blackberry
  Brandy

JERSEY LILY
  Peter Herring
  Cream

JESSICA SPECIAL
Shake and Strain
  1/2 oz Vodka
  1/2 oz Tequila
  1/2 oz Triple Sec
  Splash Orange Juice,
  Sour Mix
  Splash Cola

JEWEL BOX
Layer
  Grenadine
  Kahlua
  Banana Liqueur
  Rumple Minze

JOLLY GREEN GIANT
Shake and Strain
  1/2 oz Gin
  1/2 oz Rum
  1/2 oz Vodka
  1/2 oz G. Creme de
  Menthe
  1/2 oz Midori

JOLLY RANCHER
Shake and Strain
  1 oz Stolichnaya
  1 oz Midori
  Splash Cranberry Juice
  Splash Sour Mix

JUST FOR FUN
Layer
  Cherry Brandy
  W. Creme de Cacao

K

KAHLUA ALPHONSE
Layer
Kahlua
Cream

KAHLUA KISS
1 1/4 oz Kahlua
3/4 oz Creme de Almond
Splash Cream

KAMANIWANA LAYA
Shake and Strain
1/2 oz Myers's Dark Rum
1/2 oz Bacardi Rum
1/2 oz Amaretto
Splash Pineapple Juice

KAMIKAZE
Shake and Strain
1 1/4 oz Vodka
3/4 oz Triple Sec
Splash Rose's
Lime Juice

KANDY KANE
Layer
Creme de Almond
Peppermint Schnapps

KAYTUSHA ROCKET
Shake and Strain
1 1/4 oz 100° Vodka
3/4 oz Kahlua
Splash Pineapple Juice
Cream

KEOKI SHOOTER
Layer
Kahlua
D. Creme de Cacao
Brandy
Tia Maria

KEY LIME
MERINGUE PIE
Shake and Strain
1 1/4 oz Licor 43
3/4 oz Vodka
Splash Sour Mix
Splash Rose's
Lime Juice
Whipped Cream

KEY LIME PIE I
Shake and Strain
1 1/4 oz Licor 43
Splash Sour Mix, Rose's
Lime Juice
Splash Cream

KEY LIME PIE II
Shake and Strain
1/2 oz Vodka
1/2 oz Licor 43
1/2 Rose's Lime Juice
1/2 oz Cream

"Simply
SHOOTERS"

KILLER ALLIGATOR
Shake and Strain
- 1/2 oz Apple Schnapps
- 1/2 oz Midori
- 1/2 oz Seagram's 7
- 1/2 oz Vodka
- Splash Sour Mix, 7-Up

KILLER BEE
Layer
- Jagermeister
- Barenmeister

KILLER KAZE
Shake and Strain
- 1 1/4 oz Stolichnaya
- 3/4 oz Cointreau
- Splash Roses Lime Juice

KILLER KOOLAIDE I
Shake and Strain
- 1/2 oz Southern Comfort
- 1/2 oz Midori
- 1/2 oz Creme de Noya
- Splash Cranberry Juice

KILLER KOOLAIDE II
Shake and Strain
- Equal Parts:
- Vodka, Amaretto, Southern Comfort, Grenadine, Orange Juice, Sour Mix

KILLER PEACH
Shake and Strain
- 1 1/4 oz Peach Schnapps
- 3/4 oz Vodka

KING ALPHONSE
Layer
- D. Creme de Cacao
- Cream

KING'S CUP
Layer
- Galliano
- Cream

KIOKI SHOOTER
Layer
- Kahlua
- D. Creme de Cacao
- Brandy
- Whipped Cream

KISS IN THE DARK
Shake and Strain
- 1 3/4 oz Gin
- 3/4 oz Cherry Brandy

KITCHEN SINK
Shake and Strain
- 1 oz Orange Curacao
- 1 oz Amaretto
- Splash Orange, Pineapple Juice, Sour Mix

K

KOOLAIDE I
Shake and Strain
3/4 oz Vodka
3/4 oz Melon Liqueur
3/4 oz Creme de Almond
Splash Cranberry Juice

KOOLAIDE II
Shake and Strain
1 1/2 oz Midori Melon
Liqueur
1 oz Amaretto
Splash Cranberry Juice

KOOL FOOL
Layer
W. Creme de Menthe
Frangelico

KOOL OUT
Shake and Strain
1 1/4 Midori
3/4 Amaretto
Splash Cranberry Juice

"Simply
SHOOTERS"

L.A.P.D NIGHTSHIFT
Layer
   Grenadine
   Blue Curacao
   Tequila

L.S. SPECIAL
Layer
   Bailey's
   Grand Marnier
   Bacardi 151°

LA CUCARACHA
Rocks Glass, Cover,
Slam, Shoot
   1 1/4 oz Tequila
   3/4 oz Kahlua
   Splash Soda Water
   (No Ice)

LADYFINGER
Shake and Strain
   1 oz Gin
   1/2 oz Cherry Brandy
   1/2 oz Kirsh

LA MUSCA
Pony Glass
   Sambuca
   2 or 3 Coffee Beans

LANDSLIDE
Layer
   Banana Liqueur
   Bailey's
   Grand Marnier

LASER BEAM I
Layer
   Grenadine
   Galliano
   Tequila

LASER BEAM II
Layer
   Peppermint Schnapps
   Galliano
   Drambuie
   Wild Turkey 101°

LAYER CAKE
Layer
   Creme de Cacao
   Apricot Brandy
   Cream

LEG SPREADER I
Layer
   Kahlua
   Galliano

LEG SPREADER II
Layer
   Frangelico
   Grand Marnier

LEMON DROP I
Shake and Strain
- 1 1/4 oz Vodka
- 3/4 oz Triple Sec
- Splash Rose's
- Lime Juice
- Splash Sour Mix
- Splash Simple Syrup

LEMON DROP II
Shake and Strain
- 1 1/4 oz Vodka
- 3/4 oz Triple Sec
- Splash Lemon Juice

LEMON DROP III
Layer
- Peppermint Schnapps
- Bailey's Irish Cream
- 151° Rum
- *Flaming not recommended*

LEPRECHAUN TEA
- 1 1/4 Tequila
- 3/4 oz Green Chartreuse

LETHAL WEAPON
Shake and Strain
- 1 oz 100° Vodka
- 1 oz 151° Rum
- 1/2 oz Southern Comfort

LICORICE STICK
Shake and Strain
- 1 1/4 oz Vodka
- 3/4 oz Anisette

LIFESAVER
Shake and Strain
- 1 1/4 oz Vodka
- 3/4 oz Triple Sec
- Splash Orange Juice

LIGHTHOUSE I
Layer
- Kahlua
- Brandy
- Bacardi 151°
- *Flaming not recommended*

LIGHTHOUSE II
Layer
- Kahlua
- Gold Tequila
- 151° Rum
- *Flaming not recommended*

LION TAMER
Shake and Strain
- 1 1/4 oz Southern Comfort
- 3/4 oz Rose's
- Lime Juice

LIP LICKER
Shake and Strain
- 1 oz Kahlua
- 1/2 oz Bailey's
- 1/2 oz Amaretto

LITTLE PRINCESS
Stir and Strain
- 1 oz Rum
- 1 oz Sweet Vermouth

LITTLE PURPLE MEN
Layer
- Sambuca
- Chambord

LIZARD D___
Shake and Strain
Vodka, Southern Comfort, Midori, Sour Mix, Orange Juice, Top with 7 Up

LOBOTOMY
Layer
- Creme de Almond
- Raspberry Schnapps
- Pineapple Juice

LOLLIPOP
Shake and Strain
- 3/4 oz Cointreau
- 3/4 oz Kirsh
- 3/4 oz Green Chartreuse
- Dash Maraschino

LOUISIANA HOT SAUCE
Layer
- 1 oz Vodka
- 1 oz Tomato Juice
- 8 Drops Tabasco

LOUISIANA LOWLAND
Layer
- Kahlua
- Midori Liqueur
- Irish Cream

LUBRICATO (LUBE JOB)
Layer
- Bailey's
- Vodka

LUCAYAN SMILE
Shake and Strain
- 1 oz Dark Rum
- 1/2 oz Triple Sec
- 1/2 oz C. de Banana
- Orange Juice
- Grenadine

M-80
Layer
Cinnamon Schnapps
Vodka
Flaming not recommended

MAGGOT
Layer
G. Creme de Menthe
Bailey's Irish Cream

MALIBU EXPRESS
Layer
Frangelico
Malibu
Cream

MALIBU SHOOTER
Shake and Strain
1 1/2 oz Malibu
1/2 oz Pineapple Juice
1/2 oz Cranberry Juice
Dash Grenadine

MALTESE FALCON
Shake and Strain
Vodka , Frangelico
W. Creme de Cacao
Bailey's Irish Cream

MARMALADE
Shake and Strain
1 1/4 oz Gin
3/4 oz Triple Sec
Splash Orange Juice

MATADOR
Tequila
Pineapple

MCDLT
Amaretto
Bailey's
Tia Maria

MELLOW DRAMA
Kahlua
Irish Cream
Raspberry Liqueur

MELON BALL
Shake and Strain
1 1/4 oz Vodka
3/4 Midori
Splash Orange Juice or
Pineapple Juice

MELON POUSSE CAFE´
Layer
Creme de Almond
W. Creme de Cacao
Midori

MELON SHOOTER
Shake and Strain
1/2 oz Creme de Cassis
1/2 oz Creme de Almond
1/2 oz Southern Comfort
Splash Orange Juice
Dash Rose's
Lime Juice

MELTDOWN
Layer
Peach Schnapps
Vodka
Flaming not recommended

MEMPHIS BELLE
Layer
Southern Comfort
Irish Cream

MENAGE A TROIS
Layer
Frangelico
Melon Liqueur
Chambord
Cream

MEXICALI ROSE
Shake and Strain
1 1/4 oz Tequila
Splash Rose's
Lime Juice
Splash Cranberry Juice

MEXICAN BLIZZARD
Shake and Strain
1 1/4 oz Tequila
3/4 oz Peppermint
Schnapps

MEXICAN FLAG I
Layer
Grenadine
W. Creme de Menthe
Green Chartreuse

MEXICAN FLAG II
Layer
G. Creme de Menthe
Creme de Almond
Tequila
Flaming not recommended

MEXICAN ITCH
Layer
Tequila Gold
Mandarine Liqueur
Rose's Lime Juice

MEXICAN MISSILE
Layer
Tequila
Green Chartreuse
3 Drops Tabasco
Flaming not recommended

MEXICAN MOMMA
Layer
Tequila Gold
Licor 43

MEXICAN REVENGE
Shake and Strain
1 1/4 oz Apple Brandy
3/4 oz Tequila
Splash Orange Juice
Splash Sour Mix

MEXICAN SIESTA
Cointreau
Tequila
Sour Mix
Salt Rim, Lime

MIAMI ICE
Kahlua
Malibu
Orange Juice

MIAMI LEMONADE
Shake and Strain
1 oz Vodka
1/2 oz Triple Sec
1/2 oz Licor 43
Sour Mix, 7-Up

MIAMI VICE
Shake and Strain
1 1/4 oz Amaretto
3/4 oz Crown Royal
Splash 7-Up

MICHELLE
Shake and Strain
1 oz Peach Schnapps
1 oz Peppermint
Schnapps
Splash Orange Juice

MICK JAGGER
Shake and Strain
1 1/4 oz 100° Vodka
3/4 oz Banana Liqueur
Splash Orange Juice

MICKEY
Shake and Strain
1/2 oz Vodka
1/2 oz Amaretto
1/2 oz Grand Marnier
1/2 oz Southern
Comfort
Splash Sour Mix

MILES OF SMILES
Shake and Strain
3/4 oz Seagram's V.O.
3/4 oz C. de Almond
3/4 oz W. Creme de
Menthe

MILKY WAY
Layer
Kahlua
D. Creme de Cacao
Cream

MIND ERASER
Shake and Strain
1 1/4 oz Kahlua
3/4 oz Vodka
Splash Soda Water

MISSION ACCOMPLISHED
Shake and Strain
1 1/4 oz Vodka
3/4 oz Triple Sec
Dash Rose's Lime Juice,
Grenadine

MISSISSIPPI MUD
Shake and Strain
1 1/4 oz Kahlua
3/4 oz Southern Comfort
Splash Cream

MIXED FRUIT LIFESAVER
Layer
Creme de Banana
Blackberry Brandy

MOCHA CREAM
Shake and Strain
1 1/4 oz Kahlua
3/4 oz W. Creme de Cacao
Splash Cream

MOCHA MINT
Shake and Strain
1 oz Kahlua
1 oz W. Creme de Cacao
1 oz Creme de Menthe

MONKEY GLAND
Shake and Strain
1 1/4 oz Gin
3/4 oz Benedictine
Dash Grenadine
Splash Orange Juice

MONKEY JUICE
Shake and Strain
1 1/2 oz Malibu
Splash Orange Juice, Pineapple Juice

MONKEY'S BRAINS
Layer
Strawberry Schnapps
Bailey's Irish Cream

MONKEY'S LUNCH
Shake and Strain
1 1/4 oz Kahlua
3/4 oz Creme de Banana
Splash Myers's
Rum Cream

MONSOON
Layer
Kahlua
Creme de Almond
Irish Cream
Frangelico
Vodka
Flaming not recommended

MONTANA RATTLER
Shake and Strain
1 oz Southern Comfort
1 oz Vodka
Splash Rose's
Lime Juice

MONTE CHRISTO
1 1/2 oz Blended
Whiskey
1/2 oz Benedictine
Dash Angostura Bitters

MONTEZUMA
Shake and Strain
Tequila Gold
Whole Egg

MOONSHINE SHOOTER
Stir and Strain
1/2 oz Golden Grain
1/2 oz Gin
1/2 oz Rumple Minze

MOOSEJUICE (MILK)
Whiskey or Scotch
Cream or Milk

MOTHER LODE I
Layer
Peppermint Schnapps
Blended Whiskey

MOTHER LODE II
Shake and Strain
1 1/4 oz Canadian
Whisky
3/4 oz Peppermint
Schnapps

MOUND'S
Layer
D. Creme de Cacao
Bailey's
Malibu

MR. ED
Shake and Strain
Yukon Jack
Blue Curacao
Melon Liqueur
Orange Juice
Pineapple Juice
Rose's Lime Juice

MR. GREEN JEANS
Shake and Strain
Vodka
Malibu
Orange Juice
Pineapple Juice

MR. WILSON
Shake and Strain
Apple Schnapps
Malibu
Orange Juice
Cranberry Juice

MRS. BAILEY'S BUSH
Shake and Strain
1 oz Bailey's Irish Cream
1 oz Old Bushmills

MUD BALL
Layer
Kahlua
Bailey's
Brandy

MUD PUDDLE
Shake and Strain
1 1/4 oz Kahlua
3/4 oz Rum
Splash Orange Juice

MUD SLIDE I
Layer
1/3 oz Kahlua
1/3 oz Baileys
1/3 oz Vodka

MUD SLIDE II
Shake and Strain
3/4 oz Vodka
3/4 oz Kahlua
3/4 oz Bailey's

MUDDY WATER
Layer
Stir Once
Kahlua
Bailey's
Vodka

MULTIPLE ORGASM I
Shake and Strain
1 1/4 oz Tia Maria
3/4 oz Amaretto
Splash of Cream

MULTIPLE ORGASM II
Layer
Amaretto
Tia Maria
Cream
Vodka

MUSCLE RELAXER
Layer
Blackberry Liqueur
Southern Comfort
151° Rum
Flaming not recommended

NASHVILLE SHOOTER I

Shake and Strain
1 1/4 oz Vodka
Splash Cranberry
Juice

NASHVILLE SHOOTER II

Shake and Strain
1 1/2 oz Vodka
Sour Mix, Rose's Lime
Juice, Cranberry Juice

NAUGHTY HULA

Layer
Amaretto
D. Creme de Cacao
Cream

NEAPOM

Layer
Grand Marnier
151° Rum
Flaming not recommended

NECTARINE

1 oz Vodka
1/2 oz Peach Schnapps
Splash Cranberry Juice

NEGRONI SHOOTER

Stir and Strain
Gin, Campari,
S. Vermouth,
Soda Water

NEUTRON DEVICE (BOMB)

Stir and Strain
1 1/4 oz Vodka
3/4 oz Blue Curacao
Splash Lemon Lime
Club Soda

NEW YORK NUTHOUSE

Shake and Strain
1/4 oz Amaretto
1/4 oz Frangelico
1/4 oz Nassau Royale
1/4 oz Tia Maria
1/4 oz Vodka
1/4 oz Half & Half

NEW YORK SLAMMER I

Shake and Strain
Creme de Almond
Cointreau
Southern Comfort
Grenadine
Orange Juice

NEW YORK SLAMMER II

Shake and Strain
1/2 oz Southern Comfort
1/2 oz Amaretto
1/2 oz Triple Sec
1/2 oz Sloe Gin
1/2 oz Orange Juice

NEWPORT
Shake and Strain
1/2 oz Vodka
1/2 oz Gin
1/2 oz Rum
1/2 oz Midori
Splash Sour Mix

NICHOLAS
Shake and Strain
1 1/2 oz Vodka
3/4 oz Amaretto
Splash Cranberry Juice

NICOLASSKI
Vodka or Brandy
Lemon Wheel Over
Mouth of Glass
Sprinkle Coffee Crystals
2 Drops Triple Sec

NIGHTHAWK
Peppermint Schnapps
Myers's Dark Rum

NIGHTMARE
Shake and Strain
3/4 oz Gin
3/4 oz Red Dubonnet
1/2 oz Cherry Brandy
Splash Orange Juice

NINETY NINE (99)
Shake and Strain
3/4 oz Bailey's
3/4 oz Irish Whiskey

NINJA
Layer
Dark Creme de Cacao
Midori
Frangelico

NIPPLES
Layer
Kahlua
Sambuca
Bailey's

NO TELL MOTEL
Layer
Peppermint Schnapps
Jack Daniels

NORTH VS. SOUTH
Layer
Yukon Jack
Tequila Gold

NUCLEAR ACCELERATOR
Layer
Peppermint Schnapps
Grand Marnier
Vodka
Flaming definitely not recommended

NUCLEAR KAMIKAZE
Shake and Strain
1 1/4 oz Vodka
3/4 oz Blue Curacao
Dash Rose's Lime Juice

NUCLEAR WASTE
Shake and Strain
 1/2 oz Vodka 100°
 1/2 oz Tia Maria
 1/2 oz Amaretto
 1/2 oz Rootbeer
 Schnapps
 Splash Cream

NUTCRACKER I
Shake and Strain
 1 1/2 oz Vodka
 3/4 oz Frangelico
 Splash Cream

NUTCRACKER II
Layer
 Amaretto
 Frangelico
 Cream
 Vodka

NUTS AND BERRIES
Layer
 Frangelico
 Chambord
 Cream

NUTTY BUDDY I
Layer
 D. Creme de Cacao
 Amaretto
 Frangelico

NUTTY BUDDY II
Shake and Strain
 3/4 oz D. Creme de
 Cacao
 3/4 oz Frangelico
 Splash Cream

NUTTY IRISHMAN
Shake and Strain
 3/4 oz Bailey's
 3/4 oz Frangelico

NUTTY MONK
Shake and Strain
 1 1/4 oz Vodka
 3/4 oz Frangelico

NUTTY RUSSIAN
Shake and Strain
 3/4 oz Vodka
 3/4 oz Frangelico
 3/4 oz Bailey's

OBILIZER
Shake and Strain
- 3/4 oz Kahlua
- 3/4 oz Amaretto
- 3/4 oz Cream

ODDBALL
Shake and Strain
- 1 1/4 oz Jack Daniels
- Splash Orange Juice

OFF THE MOUTH
Shake and Strain
- 1/2 oz Vodka, Rum
- Peach Liqueur
- Dash Cream of Coconut
- Splash Pineapple,
- Cranberry Juice

OFF THE ROAD
Shake and Strain
- 1/4 oz Stolichnaya
- 1/4 Southern Comfort
- 1/4 Amaretto
- 1/4 Creme de Noya
- 1/4 oz Triple Sec
- 1/4 oz Rose's
- Lime Juice
- Splash Orange Juice
- Splash Pineapple Juice

OHIO LEMON DROP
Layer
- Galliano
- Vodka
- Place Lemon Wheel
- Over Mouth of Glass
- Sprinkle with Sugar
- Dash of 151° Rum
- Lick Sugar/Rum, Bite
- Lemon, Drink Shooter
Flaming not recommended

OHIO SHOCKER
Shake and Strain
- 3/4 oz Grand Marnier
- 3/4 oz Tia Maria
- 3/4 oz Bacardi 151°

OIL SLICK
Layer
- Rumple Minze
- Jagermeister

OLD GLORY
Layer
- Grenadine
- Peppermint Schnapps
- Creme de Yvette

OLD LAY
Shake and Strain
- 3/4 oz Tequila Gold
- 3/4 oz Cointreau
- 3/4 oz Rose's
- Lime Juice
- Dash Grenadine

ON AND OVER
Blend and Strain, Rocks Glass, On/Over Ice
  Any Blended Drink

ORANGE BLOSSOM SHOOTER
Shake and Strain
  1 1/4 oz Vodka
  Splash Orange Juice
  Dash Grenadine

ORANGE CRUSH
Shake and Strain
  1 oz Vodka
  1 oz Cointreau
  Splash Orange Juice
  Splash Soda

ORANGE OASIS
Layer
  Amaretto
  Grand Marnier
  Orange Juice, Cream

ORANGE PEEL
Shake and Strain
  3/4 oz Southern Comfort
  3/4 oz Triple Sec
  3/4 oz Bacardi

ORANGE SHERBET
  1 1/4 oz Vodka
  3/4 oz Grand Marnier
  Splash Orange Juice
  Dash Grenadine

OREO COOKIE
Layer
  D. Creme de Cacao
  Vodka
  Cream

ORGASM I
Shake and Strain
  3/4 oz Vodka
  3/4 oz Amaretto
  3/4 oz Kahlua
  Splash Cream
  (Bailey's Optional)

ORGASM II
Layer
  Kahlua
  Bailey's Irish Cream
  Amaretto
  Cream (Optional)

ORGASM III
Shake and Strain
  1/2 oz Vodka
  1/2 oz Brandy
  1/2 oz D. Creme de Cacao
  1/2 oz Amaretto
  Splash Cream

ORGASM IV
Layer
  Bailey's Irish Cream
  Peppermint Schnapps

OUT OF THE BLUE
Shake and Strain
 1 oz Vodka
 1/2 oz Blueberry
 Schnapps
 1/2 oz Blue Curacao
 Sour Mix, Club Soda

PANAMA RUM CREAM
Shake and Strain
  3/4 oz Rum
  3/4 oz Myers's
  Rum Cream
  3/4 oz Banana Liqueur

PANAMIAN REDS
Shake and Strain
  1 1/4 oz Cuervo Gold
  3/4 Cointreau
  1/2 oz Grenadine
  Splash Rose's
  Lime Juice

PANCHO VIEA
  Grenadine
  W. Creme de Menthe
  G. Creme de Menthe
  Blackberry Brandy
  Tequila Gold

PANENI
Shake and Strain
  1 oz Rum
  1/2 oz Banana Liqueur
  1/2 oz Orgeat
  Splash Orange Juice

PANGALACTIC GARGLE BLASTER
Layer
  Midori
  Light Rum
  Bacardi 151° Rum
  Flaming not recommended

PANTHER I
Shake and Strain
  1 1/2 oz Tequila
  1/2 oz Sour Mix

PANTHER II
Layer
  3/4 oz W. Creme de Menthe
  1/4 oz Peach Schnapps

PANTY DROPPER
Layer
  Kahlua
  Sloe Gin
  Vodka
  Cream

PANTY RAID
Layer
  Grenadine
  Cherry Liqueur
  Peppermint Schnapps

PARA SHOOTER
  Pear Schnapps
  Champagne

PARADISE
Shake and Strain
  1 1/4 oz Gin or Rum
  3/4 oz Apricot Brandy
  Splash Orange Juice

PEA SHOOTER
1 1/2 oz Peach Schnapps
Splash 7-Up

PEACE IN IRELAND
Layer
Irish Mist
Bailey's Irish Cream

PEACH BLAST
Layer
Peach Schnapps
Vodka
Flaming not recommended

PEACH BULLS___
Shake and Strain
1 1/4 oz Peach Schnapps
3/4 oz Chambord
1/2 oz Vodka
Splash Pineapple and Orange Juice

PEACH COBBLER
Layer
Peach Schnapps
Cinnamon Schnapp
Vodka

PEACH FUZZ
Shake and Strain
1 1/4 oz Vodka
3/4 oz Peach Schnapps
Splash Orange Juice
Splash 7-Up

PEACHES AND CREAM
Layer
Peach Schnapps
Cream
Bacardi 151° (Optional)

PEACHTREE LADY
Shake and Strain
1 1/4 oz Peach Schnapps
3/4 oz D. Creme de Cacao
Splash Cream

PEACHTREE PARTY
Layer
Peach Schnapps
Southern Comfort
Orange Juice

PEACHTREE PIRATE
Shake and Strain
1 1/4 oz Peachtree Schnapps
3/4 oz Myers's Dark Rum

PEACHTREE ROAD RACE

Shake and Strain
1 1/4 oz Vodka
3/4 oz Peachtree Schnapps
Splash Orange Juice
Splash Cranberry Juice

PEANUT BUTTER 'N JELLY

Shake and Strain
1 1/4 Frangelico
3/4 oz Blackberry Brandy

PEARL HARBOR

Shake and Strain
1 1/4 oz Vodka or Rum
3/4 oz Midori
Splash Pineapple Juice

PEARL HARBOR DAY

Shake and Strain
1/2 oz Vodka
1/2 oz Southern Comfort
1/2 oz Triple Sec
1/2 oz Creme de Noya
Splash Rose's Lime Juice
Splash Pineapple Juice

PEARL NECKLACE

Layer
W. Creme de Cacao
Cream
Vodka

PECKERHEAD

Shake and Strain
1 1/4 oz Yukon Jack
3/4 oz Amaretto
Splash Pineapple Juice

PEE WEE

Shake and Strain
1 oz Rum
1/2 oz Pear William Liqueur
Splash Pineapple Juice

PEPPERMILL

Layer
Chilled Vodka
Dash Black Pepper

PEPPERMINT PATTY

Shake and Strain
1 oz W. Creme de Menthe
1 oz D. Creme de Cacao

PERFECT JOHN??

Shake and Strain
1 1/4 oz Vodka
3/4 oz Triple Sec
1/2 oz Orange Juice

PEROQUET

1 1/4 oz Pernod
3/4 oz G. Creme de Menthe

PIN HEAD

Shake and Strain
1 1/4 oz Stolichnaya
3/4 oz Triple Sec
Splash Cranberry Juice

PINEAPPLE BOMB(ER)

Shake and Strain
1 oz Southern Comfort (or Rum)
1 oz Amaretto
Splash Pineapple Juice

PINECONE

Stir and Strain
1 oz Vodka
1/2 oz G. Creme de Menthe
1/2 oz W. Creme de Menthe

PINK HOTEL

Stir and Strain
1 oz Vodka
1/2 oz Creme de Noya
Splash 7-Up
Splash Draft Beer

PINK LEMONADE

Shake and Strain
1 1/2 oz Vodka
Splash Grapefruit Juice
Splash Cranberry Juice
Splash Sour Mix

PINK SILK PANTIES

Shake and Strain
1 1/4 oz Peach Schnapps
3/4 oz Vodka
Splash Cranberry Juice

PINK TWAT

Shake and Strain
1 1/2 oz Vodka
Splash Rose's Lime Juice
Splash Cranberry Juice
Splash Grenadine

POLAR BEAR

Shake and Strain
3/4 oz Vodka
3/4 oz D. Creme de Cacao
Splash Cola

P

POOFER

Shake and Strain
1/2 oz W. Creme de Cacao
1/2 oz Amaretto
1/2 oz Kahlua
1/2 oz Frangelico
1/2 oz Bailey's
Irish Cream
Splash Cream

POPPERS

Rocks Glass, No Ice
Cover, Slam, Drink
1 oz Any Liquor
Splash Any Carbonated
Beverage

POPSICLE I

Shake and Strain
Chambord
Frangelico
Pineapple Juice

POPSICLE II

Shake and Strain
1 1/4 oz Vodka
1/2 oz Blue Curacao
1/2 oz Pear Schnapps
Splash 7-Up

PORT AND STARBOARD

Layer
Grenadine
G. Creme de Menthe

POUSSE CAFE'

Usually any two or more liqueurs spoon floated one on top the other. Cream (Half & Half) will float (layer) on top most of the liqueurs. Liquor and high proof clear liquors may be used to top off as the last and then be set aflame. (Dangerous). This book does not recommend flaming any drink and cautions against all flaming techniques as dangerous.

POUSSE CAFE' I

Layer
Grenadine
G. Creme de Menthe
Triple Sec
Sloe Gin
Brandy (Flambe')
Flaming not recommended

POUSSE CAFE' II

Layer
  Grenadine
  W. Creme de Menthe
  Parfait Amour
  Triple Sec
  Brandy (Flambe')
  Flaming not recommended

POUSSE CAFE' III

Layer
  Grenadine
  Kahlua
  W. Creme de Menthe
  Blue Curacao
  Galliano
  Brandy

POUSSE CAFE' IV

Layer
  Kahlua
  W. Creme de Menthe
  Chambord
  Bailey's

PRAIRIE DOG

  1 1/4 oz Tequila
  5 Drops Tabasco
  Splash Tomato Juice

PRAIRIE FIRE

  1 1/2 oz Tequila
  Tabasco Sauce

PRINCESS

Layer
  Apricot Brandy
  Cream

PUFF (SLAMMER)

Cover, Slam, Drink
  1 1/4 oz Peppermint
  Schnapps
  Top With Soda Water

PUNK MONK

Shake and Strain
  1 1/4 oz Vodka
  3/4 oz Frangelico

PUPPY'S NOSE

Layer
  Peppermint Schnapps
  Tia Maria
  Baileys

PURPLE ALMOND

Shake and Strain
  3/4 oz Vodka
  3/4 oz Triple Sec
  3/4 oz Amaretto
  Splash Grape Juice
  Splash Grapefruit Juice
  Splash 7-Up

PURPLE BRANDY

Shake and Strain
  1 1/4 oz Vodka
  3/4 oz Cherry Brandy
  Splash Cream

PURPLE HAZE
Stir and Strain
> 1 1/4 oz Vodka
> 3/4 oz Chambord
> Splash 7-Up

PURPLE HEAD
Shake and Strain
> 1 1/4 oz Vodka
> 3/4 oz Triple Sec
> Splash Grape,
> Grapefruit Juice

PURPLE HOOTER (GRAPE CRUSH)
Shake and Strain
> 1 1/4 oz Vodka
> 3/4 oz Chambord
> Splash Sour Mix

PURPLE PASSION
Shake and Strain
> 1 1/4 oz Vodka
> 3/4 oz Triple Sec
> Splash Grape,
> Cranberry Juice

PURPLE RAIN
Shake and Strain
> 1 1/4 oz Vodka
> 3/4 oz Blue Curacao
> Splash Cranberry Juice

PUSSEAU PLATTER
Layer
> Kahlua
> W. Creme de Cacao
> Frangelico
> Irish Cream

QE I
Layer
  Chambord
  Gin

QE II
Layer
  Chambord
  Champagne

QUAALUDE I
Shake and Strain
  1 1/4 oz Vodka
  3/4 oz Frangelico
  Splash Cream

QUAALUDE II
Shake and Strain
  1/2 oz Vodka
  1/2 oz Southern Comfort
  1/2 oz Midori
  Dash Grenadine
  Splash Orange Juice

QUAALUDE III
Shake and Strain
  1 1/4 oz Kahlua
  1/2 oz Bailey's
  1/2 oz Vodka

QUAALUDE IV
Layer
  Bailey's
  Frangelico
  Vodka
  Flaming not recommended

QUAALUDE V
Shake and Strain
  1/2 oz Southern Comfort
  1/2 oz Midori
  1/2 oz Triple Sec
  Splash Orange Juice
  Dash Grenadine

QUAKE IN L.A.
Shake, Shake, Shake
  3/4 oz Vodka
  3/4 oz Tequila
  1/2 oz Triple Sec
  Top With Cola

QUAKE IN SAN FRAN
Shake, Shake, Shake
  3/4 oz Vodka
  3/4 oz Gin
  3/4 oz Cherry Brandy
  Top With 7-Up

QUEBEC SHOOTER
Stir and Strain
  1 1/4 oz Canadian Whisky
  3/4 oz Dry Vermouth
  1/2 oz Maraschino Liqueur

QUEEN BEE
Layer
  Galliano
  Vodka
  Flaming not recommended

QUEEN ELIZABETH II
Shake and Strain
    1 oz Royal Salute
    Scotch
    1/2 oz Nassau Royal
    Liqueur
    1/2 oz Grand Marnier
    Splash Orange Juice

QUICK CARLOS
Shake and Strain
    1 1/4 Brandy or
    Blended Whiskey
    3/4 oz Amaretto

QUICKIE
Layer
    Creme de Banana
    Blackberry Brandy
    Irish Cream

QUICKLY
Layer
    Peppermint Schnapps
    Cream

QUIET BUT QUICK
Shake and Strain
    1 1/4 Vodka
    3/4 Cherry Brandy
    Splash Orange Juice
    Dash Angostura
    Bitters

RABBIT

Shake and Strain
1 1/4 oz Southern Comfort
3/4 oz Peppermint Schnapps

RADIOACTIVE WASTE

Shake and Strain
1 oz Vodka
1/4 Each:
Melon Liqueur, Galliano, Peach Schnapps, Creme de Cassis
Orange Juice

RAGIN' CAJUN

Shake and Strain
1/2 oz Vodka
1/2 oz Southern Comfort
1/2 oz Apple Schnapps
1/2 oz Peach Schnapps
Splash Pineapple Juice
Splash Cranberry Juice

RAINBOW

Blue Curacao
G. Creme de Menthe
Peter (Cherry) Herring
Yellow Chartreuse

RAINBOW SHOOTER

Layer
Creme de Almond
Melon Liqueur
W. Creme de Cacao

RAMBO

Rocks Glass, No Ice
1/2 oz Wild Turkey 101°
1/2 oz Vodka 100°
1/2 oz Rumple Minze

RANCHO MIRAGE

Shake and Strain
1/2 oz Gin
1/2 oz Blackberry Brandy
1/2 oz Creme de Banana
Splash Cream

RASPBERRY CREAM

Shake and Strain
1 1/4 oz Vodka
3/4 oz Chambord
Splash Cream

RASPBERRY SCREAMER

Shake and Strain
1 1/4 oz Vodka
3/4 oz Raspberry Liqueur
Splash Pineapple Juice

RASPBERRY SHOOTER

Shake and Strain
1 1/4 oz Vodka
3/4 oz Chambord
Splash Orange Juice

RASPBERRY TORTE
Layer
Chambord
Absolut Vodka

RASTA MAN
Layer
D. Creme de Cacao
Tia Maria
Myers's Dark Rum

RATSASS
Shake and Strain
1 1/2 oz Gin
1/2 oz Apple Schnapps
Dash Simple Syrup
Top With 7-Up

RATTLESNAKE I
Layer
Kahlua
Bailey's
Tequila

RATTLESNAKE II
Layer
Kahlua
Peppermint Schnapps
Cream

RATTLESNAKE III
Layer
Kahlua
Amaretto
Cream

RATTLESNAKE IV
Layer
Kahlua
Banana Liqueur
Tequila

RED APPLE
Shake and Strain
1 1/4 oz Apple Schnapps
Splash Sour Mix
Dash Grenadine

RED DAIGO
Rocks Glass, No Ice
1 oz Vodka
1 oz Frangelico

RED DANE IN SWEDEN
Layer
Peter (Cherry) Herring
Absolut Vodka

RED DEATH
Stir and Strain
1 1/4 oz Vodka
3/4 oz Triple Sec
Dash Rose's Lime Juice
Dash Tabasco

RED HOT
Shake and Strain
1 1/4 oz Cinnamon Schnapps
1/2 oz Grenadine
Drops of Tabasco

RED HOT SHOOTER
Layer
Cinnamon Schnapps
3 Drops Tabasco

RED ROYAL
Shake and Strain
1 oz Crown Royal Whisky
1 oz Amaretto di Saronno

RED RUSSIAN
Shake and Strain
1 1/4 oz Stolichnaya Vodka
3/4 oz Chambord
Splash Cream

RED SILK PANTIES I
Layer
Grenadine
Cherry Brandy
Cinnamon Schnapps

RED SILK PANTIES II
Layer
Peach Schnapps
Vodka
Cranberry Juice

RED SILK PANTIES III
1 oz Stolichnaya
1 oz Peach Schnapps
Splash Cranberry Juice

RED SNAPPER I
Shake and Strain
3/4 oz Vodka
3/4 oz Kahlua
3/4 oz Amaretto
Splash Cream

RED SNAPPER II
Shake and Strain
Crown Royal
Amaretto
Cranberry Juice

RED TIGER I
Layer
Sloe Gin
Tequila
151° Rum
Flaming not recommended

RED TIGER II

Layer
- Sloe Gin
- Tequila
- Green Chartreuse
- 151° Rum

Flaming not recommended

REGGEA

Layer
- Tia Maria
- Myers's Rum Cream
- Myers's Dark Rum

RELAXING SHOOTER

Shake and Strain
- 1 oz Vodka
- 1 oz Red Wine
- Dash Simple Syrup
- Splash Cranberry Juice

RIGORMORTIS

Layer
- Amaretto
- Triple Sec
- Vodka

RIVER CLUB

Shake and Strain
- 3/4 oz Kahlua
- 3/4 oz W. Creme de Cacao
- 3/4 oz Peppermint Schnapps

ROAD RUNNER

Shake and Strain
- 3/4 oz Rum
- 3/4 oz Amaretto
- Splash Pina Colada Mix
- Splash Orange Juice

ROCK LOBSTER SHOOTER

Layer
- W. Creme de Cacao
- Irish Cream
- Cinnamon Schnapps

ROCKET FUEL I

Shake and Strain
- 1/2 oz Tequila
- 1/2 oz Cointreau
- 1/2 oz Kahlua
- 1/2 oz Amaretto
- 1/2 oz Bailey's

ROCKET FUEL II

Layer
- Rumple Minze
- 151° Bacardi

Flaming not recommended

ROLLS ROYCE

Shake and Strain
- 1 oz Cognac
- 1 oz Cointreau
- 1 oz Orange Juice

ROMAN CANDLE
Shake and Strain
1 oz Sambuca
1 oz Amaretto di Saronno
Dash Grenadine
Splash Orange Juice

ROMAN CREAM
Layer
Kahlua
Sambuca
Cream

ROMAN CREME DELIGHT
Shake and Strain
3/4 oz Kahlua
3/4 oz Sambuca
3/4 oz Galliano
Splash Cola

ROMAN HOLIDAY
Shake and Strain
3/4 oz Amaretto
3/4 oz Sambuca
3/4 oz Blackberry Brandy
Splash Cream

ROOSTER POOP
Layer
W. Creme de Menthe
Brandy
Flaming not recommended

ROOTBEER I
Shake and Strain
1 oz Vodka
1/2 oz Galliano
1/2 oz Kahlua
Splash Cola

ROOTBEER II
1 1/4 oz Kahlua
3/4 oz Galliano
Splash Cola

ROOTBEER FLOAT
1/2 oz Vodka
1/2 oz Kahlua
1/2 oz Galliano
Splash Cola
Float Cream

ROOTBEER SHOOTER
Layer
Kahlua
Galliano
Whipped Cream

ROYAL CROWN I
Shake and Strain
1 1/4 Crown Royal
3/4 oz Amaretto di Saronno
Splash Cola

R

ROYAL CROWN II
Shake and Strain
1 1/4 oz Crown Royal
3/4 oz Amaretto di Soronno
Splash 7-Up

RUM RUNNER
Shake and Strain
3/4 oz Blackberry Brandy
3/4 oz Banana Liqueur
3/4 oz Bacardi 151°
Dash Grenadine
Splash Sour Mix

RUSSIAN BEAR
Shake and Strain
1 1/4 oz Stolichnaya
3/4 oz D. Creme de Cacao
Splash Cream

RUSSIAN DEFECT
Shake and Strain
1 1/4 oz Stolichnaya
3/4 oz Peppermint Schnapps

RUSSIAN FALCON
Shake and Strain
3/4 oz Stolichnaya
3/4 oz Amaretto
3/4 oz Brandy
Splash Cream

RUSSIAN F_____
Shake and Strain
3/4 oz Stolichnaya Vodka
3/4 oz Amaretto
3/4 oz Crown Royal

RUSSIAN ICEBURG
Layer
Peppermint Schnapps
Vodka

RUSSIAN M_____ F_____
Shake and Strain
3/4 oz Stolichnaya
3/4 oz Amaretto
3/4 oz Crown Royal
3/4 oz Cuervo Gold Tequila

RUSSIAN NIGHTMARE
Shake and Strain
Jagermeister
Canadian Whisky
Peppermint Schnapps

RUSSIAN PEACH
Rocks Glass, No Ice
1 1/4 Peach Schnapps
3/4 Vodka

RUSSIAN QUAALUDE I

Shake and Strain
> 3/4 oz Stolichnaya
> Vodka
> 3/4 oz Kahlua
> 3/4 oz Frangelico
> Splash Cream

RUSSIAN QUAALUDE II

Layer
> Bailey's Irish Cream
> Grand Marnier
> Vodka
> *Flaming not recommended*

RUSTY NIPPLE

Layer
> W. Creme de Menthe
> Frangelico

S

S.O.B I
Shake and Strain
3/4 oz Bacardi 151°
3/4 Brandy
3/4 Triple Sec

S.O.B II
1 1/4 oz Cognac or
Southern Comfort
3/4 oz Cointreau

SAFE SEX ON THE BEACH
Shake and Strain
1 oz Chambord
1 oz Peach Schnapps
Splash Orange Juice

SAITO
Layer
Bailey's Irish Cream
Rumple Minze

SAMBUCA CON MUSCA
Pony Glass
Sambuca
3 Coffee Beans

SAVOY HOTEL
Layer
W. Creme de Cacao
Benedictine
Brandy

SCHNAPPS SLAMMER
Rocks Glass, No Ice
Cover, Slam, Drink
2 oz Schnapps (Any)
Splash Club Soda

SCREAMER
Layer
Metaxa
G. Chartreuse

SCREAMING APPLE
Shake and Strain
1 oz Vodka
1 oz Apple Schnapps

SCREAMING CRANAPPLE
Shake and Strain
1 1/4 oz Vodka
3/4 oz Apple Schnapps
Splash Cranberry Juice

SCREAMING HORNEY MONKEY
Shake and Strain
3/4 oz Vodka
3/4 oz Kahlua
3/4 oz Banana Liqueur
Splash Cream

SCREAMING ORGASM

Shake and Strain
1/2 oz Vodka or Tequila
1/2 oz Kahlua
1/2 oz Amaretto
1/2 oz Bailey's
Irish Cream

SCREAMING PEACHTREE

Shake and Strain
3/4 oz Vodka
3/4 oz Peach Schnapps
Splash Orange Juice
Splash Cream

SCREAMING SEX ON THE BEACH

Shake and Strain
3/4 oz 100° Vodka
3/4 oz Peach Schnapps
3/4 oz Chambord
Splash Orange,
Cranberry Juice

SEA HAWK

Shake and Strain
Vodka
Blue Curacao
Melon Liqueur

SEPARATOR

1 1/4 oz Brandy
3/4 oz Kahlua
Splash Cream

SERGEANT PRESTON

Layer
Yukon Jack
Irish Cream

SEVEN FORTY SEVEN (747)

Layer
Kahlua
Bailey's
Frangelico

SEVEN FOURTEEN (714)

Layer
Tia Maria
Bailey's
Grand Marnier

SEVEN TWENTY SEVEN (727)

Shake and Strain
1/2 oz Vodka
1/2 oz Kahlua
1/2 oz Grand Marnier
1/2 oz Bailey's
Irish Cream

SEX

Shake and Strain
1 oz Kahlua
1 oz Grand Marnier

SEX AT MY HOUSE
Layer
Creme de Noyaux
Raspberry Liqueur
Pineapple Juice

SEX AT THE BEACH
Shake and Strain
1/2 oz Vodka
1/2 oz Peach Schnapps
1/2 oz Apple Schnapps
1/2 oz Grand Marnier
1/2 oz Southern Comfort
Splash Orange,
Cranberry, Cream

SEX MACHINE
Shake and Strain
1/2 oz Vodka
1/2 oz Kahlua
1/2 oz Grand Marnier
Float Cream

SEX ON THE BAR
Shake and Strain
3/4 oz Vodka
3/4 oz Peach Schnapps
3/4 oz Chambord
Splash Orange,
Cranberry Juice

SEX ON THE BEACH I
Shake and Strain
1 1/2 oz Peach
Schnapps
Splash Cranberry Juice

SEX ON THE BEACH II
Shake and Strain
1 1/4 oz Midori
3/4 oz Chambord
Splash Orange or
Pineapple Juice
Splash Sour Mix

SEX ON THE BEACH III
Shake and Strain
Vodka
Chambord
Peach Schnapps
Orange Juice,
Cranberry Juice

SEX ON THE BEACH IV
Vodka
Chambord
Orange Juice
Cranberry Juice

SEX ON THE BEACH V
Shake and Strain
Vodka
Chambord
Tia Maria
Pineapple Juice

SEX ON THE BEACH (FLA)
Shake and Strain
Vodka
Midori
Peach Schnapps
Pineapple Juice

SEX ON THE BEACH (NY)
Shake and Strain
Vodka
Peach Schnapps
Chambord (Optional)
Orange Juice
Cranberry Juice

SEX ON THE BEACH (ORIGINAL)
Shake and Strain
1 Part Chambord
2 Parts Midori
3 Parts Pineapple Juice

SEX ON THE BEACH FOR A WEEK
Shake and Strain
Vodka
Midori
Cranberry Juice
Pineapple Juice

SEX ON THE ROCKS
Layer
Kahlua
Grand Marnier
Cream

SEXY
Layer
Kahlua
Amaretto

SHALALEY
Layer
G. Creme de Menthe
Bailey's Irish Cream
Vodka
Flaming not recommended

SHAMROCK
Shake and Strain
1 1/4 oz Irish Whiskey
1/2 oz Dry Vermouth
1/2 oz Green Chartreuse
1/2 oz G. Creme de Menthe

SHARK SHOOTER
Build, Rocks Glass
   Vodka, Chambord,
   Triple Sec
   Orange Juice
   Champagne

SHARK'S TOOTH I
Shake and Strain
   3/4 oz Cuervo Gold
   3/4 Midori
   Splash Sour Mix

SHARK'S TOOTH II
Layer
   100° Vodka
   Cream

SHAVING BRUSH (SHAVED BUSH)
Shake and Strain
   1/2 oz Rum
   1/2 oz Amaretto
   1/2 oz W. Creme de Cacao
   1/2 oz Kahlua
   Splash Cream

SHIT KICKER (SHIT SHOOTER)
Shake and Strain
   3/4 oz Crown Royal
   3/4 oz Amaretto
   3/4 oz Peppermint Schnapps

SHOGUN SHOOTER
Layer
   Melon Liqueur (Midori)
   Vodka

SHOT IN THE DARK
Layer
   Yukon Jack
   Orange Curacao
   Tia Maria

SICILIAN KISS
Shake and Strain
   1 1/4 oz Southern Comfort
   3/4 oz Amaretto

SILK
Shake and Strain
   1 oz Cognac
   1 oz Grand Marnier
   Splash Cream

SILK PANTIES
   W. Creme de Cacao
   Triple Sec
   Gin
   Cream

SILK PANTY
Shake and Strain
   1 1/4 oz Vodka
   3/4 oz Peach Schnapps
   Splash Cranberry Juice (Optional)

SILK PINK PANTIES
Layer
   Grenadine
   W. Creme de Cacao
   Cream
   Gin

SILVER BULLET
Shake and Strain
   1 1/4 oz 100° Vodka
   3/4 oz Peppermint
   Schnapps or Bailey's

SILVER CLOUD
Shake and Strain
   1 oz Kahlua
   1 oz Amaretto
   Splash Cream

SILVERY BISCUIT
Shake and Strain
   3/4 oz Smirnoff Silver
   Vodka
   3/4 oz Frangelico
   3/4 oz Bailey's

SIT DOWN AND SHUT UP!
Shake and Strain
   3/4 oz Blackberry
   Brandy
   3/4 oz Southern Comfort
   3/4 oz Peppermint
   Schnapps

SIT SALLY!!
Shake and Strain
   3/4 oz Blended Whiskey
   3/4 oz Frangelico
   3/4 oz Irish Cream

SKI LODGE
Layer
Snifter, No Ice
   Grand Marnier
   B&B

SKIP AND GO NAKED
Shake and Strain
   1 oz Gin
   Splash Sour Mix
   Dash Grenadine or
   Orange Juice
   Splash Beer

SLAM DUNK
Cover, Slam, Shoot
   1 1/4 oz Tequila
   Dash Rose's
   Lime Juice
   Dash Soda

SLAM YO MAMA
Shake and Strain
   1/2 oz Myers's Dark Rum
   1/2 oz Apple Schnapps
   1/2 oz Peach Schnapps
   1/2 oz Cherry Brandy
   Splash Cranberry Juice
   Splash Sour Mix

SLAMMERS

Rocks Glass, No Ice
Cover, Slam, Drink
    1 1/2 - 2 oz Any
    Liquor
    Splash Any
    Carbonated Mixer

SLAP SHOT

Layer
    Peppermint Schnapps
    Southern Comfort

SLIPPERY BUBBLE

Layer
    Sambuca
    Irish Cream

SLIPPERY D___

Layer
    Amaretto
    Bailey's or Peppermint
    Schnapps
    (Your Choice)

SLIPPERY KNOB

Shake and Strain
    1 1/4 oz Vodka
    3/4 oz Grand Marnier

SLIPPERY NIPPLE I (LEFT)

Layer
    Sambuca
    Bailey's

SLIPPERY NIPPLE II (RIGHT)

Layer
    Peppermint Schnapps
    Bailey's
    Amaretto (Optional)

SLIPPERY NIPPLE III

    W. Creme de Cacao
    Bailey's
    Whipped Cream

SLIPPERY T__

Layer
    Kahlua
    Peppermint
    Bailey's

SMOKEY MOUNTAIN WHITETOP

Shake and Strain
    1 1/4 oz Vodka
    3/4 oz Tia Maria
    Float Cream

SMOOTHIE

Shake and Strain
    1 1/4 oz Vodka
    3/4 oz Orange Curacao
    Splash Orange Juice

SMURF SHOOTER

Shake and Strain
    1 1/4 oz Vodka
    3/4 oz Blue Curacao
    Dash Rose's Lime Juice

S

SNAKE BIT
Shake and Strain
1 1/4 oz Wild
Turkey 101°
3/4 oz Peppermint
Schnapps

SNAKEBITE I
Shake and Strain
1 1/4 oz Yukon Jack
3/4 oz Rose's
Lime Juice

SNAKEBITE II
Peppermint Schnapps
Canadian Club

SNAKEBITE III
Peppermint Schnapps
Chartreuse Green

SNICKERS
D. Creme de Cacao
Bailey's
Frangelico
Cream

SNOW CAP
Bailey's
Tequila

SNOW CRAB
W. Creme de Cacao
Bailey's
2 or 3 Drops Peppermint
Schnapps

SNOW SHOE I
Shake and Strain
1 1/4 oz Wild
Turkey 101°
3/4 oz Peppermint
Schnapps

SNOW SHOE II
Layer
Peppermint Schnapps
Southern Comfort

SOLAR CELL
Shake and Strain
Scotch
Drambuie
Triple Sec

SOLAR POWER
Layer
Triple Sec
Drambuie
Scotch

SOM-BITCH
Layer
Southern Comfort
151° Rum
Flaming not recommended

SOUL KISS
Shake and Strain
1 oz Blended Whiskey
1/2 oz Dry Vermouth
1/2 oz Dubonnet
Splash Orange Juice

SOUR GRAPES
Shake and Strain
Vodka
Chambord
Sour Mix

SOUTH OF THE BORDER SHOT
1 oz Tequila
Lime Wedge, Salt

SOUTHERN ANGEL
Layer
Southern Comfort
Amaretto
Bacardi 151°
Flaming not recommended

SOUTHERN BITCH
Shake and Strain
Equal Parts: Southern Comfort, Peach Brandy, Amaretto, Splash Orange Juice, Cranberry Juice, Pineapple Juice

SOUTHERN FLAME
1 1/2 oz Southern Comfort
1/2 oz Bacardi 151°
Flaming not recommended

SPANISH FLY
Shake and Strain
1 1/4 oz Tequila
3/4 oz Amaretto

SPERM BANK I
Layer
Kahlua
Bailey's
W. Creme de Cacao
Amaretto
Drop Grenadine

SPERM BANK II
W. Creme de Menthe
Vodka

SPERM BANK DEPOSIT
Layer
Cuervo Gold Tequila
Drop Cream

SPIKE
Shot Glass, No Ice
Tequila
Grapefruit Juice

ST. MORITZ
Chambord
Cream

ST. PAT
3/4 oz Irish Whiskey
3/4 oz G. Chartreuse
3/4 G. Creme de Menthe

ST. THOMAS SPECIAL
Shake and Strain
 1 1/4 oz Rum
 3/4 oz Peter Herring
 Splash Cream

STARBOARD LIGHTS I
Layer
 Vodka
 G. Creme de Menthe
 151° Bacardi
 Flaming not recommended

STARBOARD LIGHTS II
Layer
 G. Creme de Menthe
 Galliano
 151° Rum
 Flaming not recommended

STARS AND STRIPES I
Layer
 Blackberry Brandy With
 Blue Curacao
 Peppermint Schnapps
 Southern Comfort
 Flaming not recommended

STARS AND STRIPES II
 Grenadine
 Maraschino
 Parfait Amour

STARS AND STRIPES III
Layer
 Grenadine
 Peppermint Schnapps
 Creme de Yvette

STARS AND STRIPES IV
Layer
 Grenadine
 Cream
 Blue Curacao

STEEL BALLS
Layer
 Midori
 100° Vodka
 Flaming not recommended

STEELY DAN
Shake and Strain
 1 1/2 oz Tequila
 Splash Ginger Ale

STERNO SHOOTER
Layer
 Blue Curacao
 Bacardi 151°
 Flaming not recommended

STIFF D___
Layer
 Bailey's
 Butterscotch Schnapps

S

STOLI BUSTER
Shake and Strain
- 1 oz Stolichnaya Vodka
- 1 oz Bailey's Irish Cream

STONE BANANA
Shake and Strain
- 1/2 oz Vodka
- 1/2 oz Kahlua
- 1/2 oz Amaretto
- 1/2 Banana Liqueur
- Splash Cream

STONE SOUR
Shake and Strain
- Southern Comfort
- Orange Juice
- Sour Mix

STOPLIGHT I
Bottom Glass	1/2 oz Vodka
	1/2 oz Midori
Middle Glass	1/2 oz Vodka
	Orange Juice
Top Glass	1/2 oz Vodka
	Cranberry Juice

Stack The Three
Separate Rocks Glasses
On One Another

STOPLIGHT II
Layer
- G. Creme de Menthe
- Creme de Banana
- Creme de Almond or
- Sloe Gin

STORM CLOUD I
Shake and Strain
- 1 1/4 oz Frangelico
- 3/4 oz Bacardi 151°
- 3 Drops Cream

STORM CLOUD II
Layer
- Kahlua
- Bacardi 151°
- *Flaming not recommended*

STORM CLOUD III
Swirl and Strain
- 1 1/4 oz Bailey's
- 3/4 oz Amaretto
- Dash Bacardi 151°
- Splash Cream After
- Strain

STRAIGHT SHOOTER
Layer
- Galliano
- Sweet Vermouth

"Simply **SHOOTERS"**

STRAWBERRY BLOND
Layer
  Grenadine
  D. Creme de Cacao
  Bailey's

STRAWBERRY SHORTCAKE
Shake and Strain
  3/4 oz Amaretto
  3/4 oz Strawberry Liqueur
  3/4 oz Grenadine
  Splash Cream
  Whipped Cream

STRAWBETTY
Layer
  Strawberry Liqueur
  Amaretto
  Whipped Cream

STUPID SHOOTER
Shake and Strain
  3/4 oz Crown Royal
  3/4 oz Amaretto
  3/4 oz Southern Comfort

SUMMER DELIGHT
Shake and Strain
  3/4 oz Chambord
  3/4 oz Midori
  3/4 oz Vodka
  Splash Cream,
  Pineapple Juice

SUMMIT
Shake and Strain
  1 1/4 oz Vodka
  3/4 oz Blackberry Brandy

SUNBEAM I
  1 1/4 oz Galliano
  3/4 oz Sweet Vermouth

SUNBEAM II
Layer
  Galliano
  Dry Vermouth

SUNKIST
Stir and Strain
  1 1/4 oz Vodka
  3/4 oz Triple Sec
  Splash Orange Juice
  Splash Soda Water

SUZY Q
Shake and Strain
  Apricot Brandy
  Creme de Banana
  D. Creme de Cacao
  Cranberry Juice

SWAMPWATER
Shake and Strain
  1 1/4 oz Vodka
  3/4 oz Midori or
  Green Chartreuse
  Splash Pineapple Juice

SWEDISH QUAALUDE
Shake and Strain
  3/4 oz Absolut Vodka
  3/4 oz Frangelico
  3/4 oz Bailey's

SWEET PEACH
Shake and Strain
  3/4 oz Amaretto
  3/4 oz Peach Schnapps
  Splash Orange Juice

SWEET TART
Shake and Strain
  1 1/4 oz Rum
  3/4 oz Chambord
  1/2 oz Sour Mix
  Dash Rose's Lime Juice
  Top With 7-Up

SWITCHBLADE
Shake and Strain
  1 1/2 oz Gin
  1/2 oz Triple Sec
  Dash Rose's Lime Juice

T-BIRD
Layer
 Vodka
 Amaretto
 Grand Marnier
 Pineapple Juice
 Cream (Optional)

T.K.O. I
Shake and Strain
 3/4 oz Tequila Gold
 3/4 oz Kahlua
 3/4 oz Anisette or Ouzo

T.K.O II
 T = Tequila
 K = Kahlua
 O = Ouzo

TNT SHOOTER
Rocks Glass, No Ice
 Tequila
 Tonic Water

T&T
Shake and Strain
 1 1/4 oz Tequila
 3/4 oz Tia Maria

TAMPA BAY SMOOTHIE
Shake and Strain
 Vodka
 Triple Sec
 Orange Juice
 Grenadine

TASMANIAN
Rocks Glass, No Ice
 1 1/2 oz Capt.
 Morgan's Rum
 Grenadine
 Splash 7 Up

TEAR DROP
Layer
 Vodka
 Grand Marnier

TEDDY BEAR
Layer
 Root Beer Schnapps
 Vodka

TEQUILA PRETTY GIRL
 Tequila Gold
 Side Lime Wedge, Salt

TEQUILA PUFF SLAMMER
Rocks Glass, No Ice
Cover, Slam, Drink
 1 1/2 oz Tequila
 Dash Rose's Lime Juice
 Splash Ginger Ale or
 Splash 7-Up

TEQUILA SLAMMER
Rocks Glass, No Ice
Cover, Slam, Drink
 Tequila
 Splash 7-Up

TEST TUBE BABY
I, II, III, IV, V
I Southern Comfort,
Sambuca
II Wild Turkey,
Peppermint Schnapps
III Tequila, Amaretto
IV Tequila, Kahlua
V Wild Turkey,
Grand Marnier
Drop of One: Bailey's,
Grenadine or Cream,
Use a Straw

TEXAS SWEAT
Layer
1/2 oz Grenadine
1/2 oz G. Creme de
Menthe
Dash Tequila
Dash 151° Rum
Flaming not recommended

TEXAS WATERMELON
Shake and Strain
Southern Comfort
Creme de Almond
Orange Juice
Pineapple Juice

THE THRILLER
Layer
Strawberry Liqueur
Drambuie
Bacardi 151°
Flaming not recommended

THIRTY ONE FLAVORS
Layer
Kahlua
Banana Liqueur
D. Creme de Cacao
Cream

THIS AND THAT
Snifter, No Ice
1 oz Cognac
1 oz Grand Marnier

THREE MUSKETEERS
Shake and Strain
Tia Maria
D. Creme de Cacao
Cream

THRILLER
Layer
Kahlua
Bailey's
Crown Royal
Flaming not recommended

THUMPER
Snifter or Pony
Tuaca
Brandy

THUNDER AND
LIGHTENING
Layer
Rumple Minze
151° Rum
Flaming not recommended

TIDAL WAVES
Shake and Strain
   3/4 oz Vodka
   3/4 oz Myers's Dark Rum
   Sour Mix
   Cranberry Juice

TIDY BOWL
Shake and Strain
   1 1/4 oz Vodka
   3/4 oz Blue Curacao
   Splash Sour Mix

TIGER'S MILK
Layer
   Tuaca
   Cream

TIJUANA TIT TICKLER
Layer
   Triple Sec
   Tuaca
   Tequila
   Flaming not recommended

TINY DANCER
Shake and Strain
   3/4 oz Vodka
   3/4 oz Frangelico
   3/4 oz Cuarenta y Tres
   (Liqor 43)

TIT
Layer
   Tia Maria
   Cream

TOM – O'SHANTER
Shake and Strain
   1 oz Irish Whiskey
   1 oz Kahlua
   Float Cream

TOMA – KAZI
Shake and Strain
   3/4 oz Gin
   3/4 oz Vodka
   3/4 oz Triple Sec
   Dash Rose's Lime Juice

TOOTSIE ROLL SHOOTER
Shake and Strain
   1 1/2 oz D. Creme de Cacao
   Splash Orange Juice

TORPEDO
Shake and Strain
   1 1/4 oz Vodka
   Splash Bloody Mary Mix

TORQUE WRENCH
Layer
   Melon Liqueur
   Orange Juice
   Champagne

TOWERING INFERNO
Layer
Kahlua
Wild Turkey
Brandy
Cream

TOXIC WASTE
Shake and Strain
Vodka
Midori
Yukon Jack
Sour Mix
Cranberry Juice

TRAFFIC LIGHT (STOP LIGHT)
Layer
Sloe Gin
Creme de Banana
G. Creme de Menthe

TRANSFUSION
Stir and Strain
Vodka
Red Wine
Splash 7-Up

TREE CLIMBER
Shake and Strain
3/4 oz Amaretto
3/4 oz W. Creme de Cacao
3/4 oz Cream

TRIFECTA
Layer
Creme de Banana
Irish Cream
Rum
Drops Cream

TROPICAL LIFESAVER
Layer
Grenadine
Cherry Liqueur
Galliano
Triple Sec

TRUE PEACH
Shake and Strain
1 oz Vodka
1 oz Peach Schnapps
Dash Grenadine
Splash Orange, Grapefruit, Pineapple Juice

TUACA POUSSE CAFE´
Layer
Grenadine
W. Creme de Cacao
Midori
Tuaca

TURKEY SHOOTER
Layer
Peppermint Schnapps
Wild Turkey 101°
Flaming not recommended

TURKEY TROT
Layer
  Wild Turkey Liqueur
  Wild Turkey 101°
  Flaming not recommended

TUSH PUSH SHOOTER
Shake and Strain
  Rum
  Creme de Cassis
  Cointreau
  Dash Rose's Lime Juice
  Dash Orange Juice,
  Pineapple Juice

TWO FIFTY TWO 252
Layer
  Wild Turkey 101°
  Bacardi Rum 151°
  Flaming not recommended

TYCOON
Shot Glass
  1 oz 1800 Gold Tequila
  Lime Squeeze, Salt

U – Z (UZI)
Shake and Strain
- 3/4 oz Irish Mist
- 3/4 oz Irish Cream
- 1/4 oz Kahlua

UKRANIAN SHOOTER
Layer
- Kahlua
- Grand Marnier
- Amaretto
- Whipped Cream
- 3 Drops Tia Maria

UNCLE SAM
Layer
- Parfait Amour
- Cherry Brandy
- Cream

UNDERGRADUATE SHOOTER
Shot Glass, No Ice
- 1/2 oz Seagram's 7
- 1/2 oz 7-Up

UNION JACK
Layer
- Grenadine
- Maraschino
- Green Chartreuse

UNITED WE STAND SHOOTER
Rocks Glass, No Ice
- 3/4 oz Bourbon
- 3/4 oz Blended Whiskey
- Splash 7-Up

UNIVERSAL
Shake and Strain
- 1 1/4 oz Vodka
- 3/4 oz Midori
- Splash Grapefruit Juice

UPSIDE DOWN MARGARITA
Shake and Strain
Into Open Mouth
- 1 oz Tequila
- 1/2 oz Triple Sec
- 1 oz Sour Mix
Caution:
May cause choking
Not recommended

UPSY DAISY SHOOTER
Layer
- Cherry Brandy
- Vodka
- 3 or 4 Drops Rose's
- Lime Juice

URINALYSIS
Layer
- W. Creme de Menthe
- Southern Comfort

V.O. BREEZE

Shake and Strain
3/4 oz V.O.
3/4 oz W. Creme de Menthe
Dash Grenadine

VELVET DREAM

Layer
Black Velvet
Triple Sec
Rose's Lime Juice

VELVET GLOVE SHOOTER

Shake and Strain
1 1/4 oz Sloe Gin
3/4 oz W. Creme de Cacao
Splash Cream

VESUVIUS

Layer
D. Creme de Cacao
Green Chartreuse
Flaming not recommended

VOLCANO

Layer
Kahlua
Bailey's
Grand Marnier
151° Rum
Flaming not recommended

VOODOO DEATH SHOT

Layer
Blackberry Brandy
Creme de Banana
151° Rum
Flaming not recommended

VOODOO SHOOTER

Layer
Coffee Liqueur
Myers's Rum Cream
151° Bacardi Rum
Flaming not recommended

VULCAN MIND PROBE

Layer
Bailey's
Midori
151° Rum
Flaming not recommended

WANDERING MINSTRAL

Shake and Strain
   1/2 oz Vodka
   1/2 oz Brandy
   1/2 oz W. Creme de
   Cacao (or Menthe)
   1/2 oz Kahlua

WARM FUZZY

Layer
   Amaretto
   151° Bacardi
   Flaming not recommended

WATERGATE

Layer
   Kahlua
   Myers's Rum Cream
   Peppermint Schnapps
   Grand Marnier

WATERMELON I

Shake and Strain
   3/4 oz Southern Comfort
   3/4 oz Amaretto
   3/4 oz Creme de Almond
   Splash Orange Juice,
   Cranberry Juice

WATERMELON II

Shake and Strain
   1 oz Vodka
   1 oz Southern Comfort
   Dash Grenadine
   Splash Pineapple Juice

WATERMELON III

Shake and Strain
   1 1/4 oz Southern
   Comfort
   3/4 oz Creme de
   Almond
   Splash Pineapple or
   Orange Juice

WEEK AT THE BEACH I

Shake and Strain
   1 oz Peach Schnapps
   1 oz Apple Schnapps
   Splash Orange Juice,
   Cranberry Juice

WEEK AT THE BEACH II

Shake and Strain
   1/2 oz Vodka
   1 oz Peach Schnapps
   Splash Cranberry Juice,
   Orange Juice

WEEK ON THE BEACH

Shake and Strain
   3/4 oz Vodka
   3/4 oz Peach Schnapps
   3/4 oz Apple Schnapps
   Splash Pineapple Juice,
   Orange Juice, Cranberry
   Juice, Grenadine

W

WEEKEND AT THE BEACH
Shake and Strain
3/4 oz Vodka
3/4 oz Peach Schnapps
3/4 oz Apple Schnapps
Splash Orange,
Grapefruit, Cranberry
Juice

WET DREAMS I
Bailey's Irish Cream
Raspberry Schnapps
Cream

WET DREAMS II
Shake and Strain
1 1/4 Malibu
3/4 Creme de Almond
Splash Pineapple Juice

WET DREAMS III
Layer
Kahlua
Bailey's
Amaretto
Cream
Vodka
Flaming not recommended

WET DREAMS IV
Shake and Strain
3/4 oz Chambord
3/4 oz Banana Liqueur
Splash Orange Juice
Splash Cream

WHAT CRISIS?
Shake and Strain
3/4 oz Peach Schnapps
3/4 Melon Liqueur
Splash Cranberry,
Orange Juice

WHISPER
Layer
Kahlua
Amaretto
Vodka
Cream

WHITE CACTUS
Shake and Strain
1 1/2 oz Tequila
Splash 7-Up
Dash Rose's Lime Juice

WHITE CROSS
Layer
1/4 W Creme de Cacao
3/4 W Creme. de Menthe

WHITE GLOVES
Shake and Strain
1 1/4 Vodka
3/4 W Creme de Cacao
Splash Cream

WHITE LADY
Shake and Strain
3/4 Brandy
3/4 Cointreau
3/4 W Creme de Menthe

WHITE LIGHTENING
Shake and Strain
1 1/4 oz Tequila
3/4 oz Peppermint
Schnapps

WHITE SHEET
Layer
1/4 W Creme de Cacao
3/4 W C. de Menthe

WHITE SPIDER SHOOTER
Shake and Strain
1 1/4 oz Vodka
3/4 W Creme de Menthe

WHITE SWAN
Shake and Strain
1 1/2 oz Amaretto
Splash Cream

WHITE WING
Shake and Strain
1 1/4 oz Gin
3/4 W Creme de Menthe

WHITE WITCH
Shake and Strain
1 1/4 oz Bailey's
3/4 oz Grand Marnier

WILD HAWAIIAN TURKEY SHOOTER
Shake and Strain
3/4 oz Southern Comfort
3/4 oz Wild Turkey 101°
3/4 oz Amaretto
Splash Pineapple,
Orange Juice

WILLY
Shake and Strain
1 1/4 oz Vodka
3/4 oz Frangelico
Dash Rose's Lime Juice

WINDEX
Shake and Strain
3/4 oz Vodka
3/4 oz Blue Curacao
3/4 oz Rum
Dash Rose's Lime Juice

WOMBAT
Shake and Strain
2 oz Dark Rum
1/2 oz Grenadine
Splash Pineapple Juice,
Orange Juice

WONDERFUL
Shake and Strain
3/4 oz Cognac
3/4 oz Grand Marnier
3/4 oz Amaretto

W

WOO WOO
Shake and Strain
1 1/4 oz Vodka
3/4 oz Peach Schnapps
Splash Cranberry Juice

WOOF PUSSEAU
Shake and Strain
1 oz Wild Turkey 101°
1 oz Frangelico

WORKING AT THE BEACH
Shake and Strain
1 oz Vodka
1/2 oz Cherry Brandy
1/2 oz Frangelico
Splash Pineapple Juice,
Orange Juice

X

X GENERATION
Layer
   Grenadine
   Creme de Banana
   151° Rum
   Flaming not recommended

X LAX SHOOTER
Layer
   Kahlua
   D. Creme de Cacao

XMAS I
Layer
   Creme de Almond
   Green Chartreuse
   Flaming not recommended

XMAS II
Layer
   Grenadine
   G. Creme de Menthe

XTRA SHOT
Layer
   G. Creme de Menthe
   Peppermint Schnapps

XTRA VERT SHOOTER
Stir and Strain
   Rumple Minze
   Frangelico

XTRA XTRA VERT
Layer
   Frangelico
   Peppermint Schnapps
   Brandy
   Flaming not recommended

"Simply SHOOTERS"

YELLOW BIRD I
Shake and Strain
- 3/4 oz Rum
- 3/4 oz Banana Liqueur
- 3/4 oz Galliano
- Splash Orange Juice

YELLOW BIRD II
Shake and Strain
- 1 1/4 oz Rum
- 1/2 oz Triple Sec
- 1/2 oz Galliano
- Splash Orange Juice

YELLOW BRICK ROAD
Shake and Strain
- 1 1/4 oz Southern Comfort
- 3/4 Amaretto
- Splash Orange Juice

YELLOW MONKEY
Shake and Strain
- 1/2 Golden Rum
- 1/2 Galliano
- 12 W Creme de Cacao
- 1/2 Creme de Banana
- 1/2 Cream

YELLOW PARROT
Shake and Strain
- 1 oz Apricot Brandy
- 1/2 oz Yellow Chartreuse
- 1/2 oz Ouzo or Anisette

YOG
- Yukon Jack
- Orange Juice
- Grapefruit Juice

YOUNGSTER SLAMMER
Rocks Glass, No Ice
Cover, Slam, Drink
- 1 1/2 oz Sloe Gin
- Splash 7-Up

YURAFUKA
Shake and Strain
- 1 oz Yukon Jack
- 1 oz Southern Comfort
- Splash Pineapple Juice

Z

Z STREET SLAMMER
Shake and Strain
Rocks Glass, No Ice
Cover, Slam, Drink
  1 oz Myers's Dark Rum
  1/2 oz C. de Banana
  Dash Grenadine
  Splash Pineapple Juice
  Splash Club Soda

ZAMMY SHOOTER
Shake and Strain
  1 1/4 oz Vodka
  3/4 oz C. de Cassis
  Splash Pineapple Juice,
  Orange Juice

ZIPPED LIP
Layer
  Grenadine
  Blackberry Brandy
  Vodka
  Flaming not recommended

ZIPPY
Shake and Strain
  1 oz D. C. de Cacao
  1 oz Bailey's Irish Cream
  3 Drops Tabasco

ZOMBIE'S KID BROTHER
Shake and Strain
  1/2 oz Dark Rum
  1/2 oz C. de Almond
  1/2 oz Triple Sec
  Splash Sour Mix,
  Orange Juice
  Top with 151° Rum
  Flaming not recommended

ZOOM SHOOTER
Shake and Strain
  Vodka
  Triple Sec
  Orange Juice
  Grapefruit Juice
  Grenadine

ZORBA
Shake and Strain
  1 1/4 oz Metaxa
  3/4 oz Amaretto

ZZUU (THAT IS ALL!)
Rock Glass, No Ice
Sip and Relax
  Ice Cold Water

"Simply
SHOOTERS"

BAM BINO
Shake and Strain
- 1 oz Vodka
- 3/4 oz Triple Sec
- 1/2 oz Rose's Lime Juice

BANANA RUMA
Shake and Strain
- 1/2 oz Rum
- 1 oz Creme de Banana
- Splash Orange, Pineapple Juice

BART SIMPSON
Layer
- Malibu
- Melon Liqueur
- Vodka
Flaming not recommended

BETTER THAN SEX
Shake and Strain
- 1 oz Vodka
- 1/2 oz Raspberry Liqueur
- 1/2 oz Sour Mix

BLUE LEMON-AIDE
Shake and Strain
- 1 oz Vodka or Rum
- 3/4 oz Blue Curacao
- Splash Sour Mix

BLUE NUTS
Shake and Strain
- 1/2 oz Vodka
- 1/2 oz Blueberry Schnapps
- 1/2 oz Blue Curacao
- Splash Cranberry Juice

BODY CHEMISTRY
Shake and Strain
- 1 oz Vodka
- 1/2 oz Southern Comfort
- 1/2 oz Cranberry Juice
- Dash Rose's Lime Juice

BOOGER
Layer
- Peach Schnapps
- 5 Drops Irish Cream

BUTTERY NIPPLE
Layer
- 1 oz Buttershots Liqueur
- 1/2 oz Bailey's Irish Cream

CALIFORNIA MOTHER
Shake and Strain
- Brandy
- Kahlua
- Bailey's
- Splash Cola
- Top with Tequila

STOP THE PRESS! RECIPE ADDENDUM

CHOCOLATE ORGASM
Layer
  D. Creme de Cacao
  Amaretto
  Bailey's
  Whipped Cream

CRANIUM MELTDOWN
Shake and Strain
  1/2 oz Each: Malibu,
  Myers's Dark Rum,
  Raspberry Liqueur,
  Pineapple Juice

DELIRIOUS
Shake and Strain
  Equal Parts: Rum,
  Peach Brandy
  Orange, Pineapple Juice

DICK N' CIDER
Rocks Glass, No Ice
  George Dickel
  Tenn. Whiskey
  Apple Cider or Juice

FIREWATER
Layer
  Peppermint Schnapps
  Cinnamon Schnapps
  151° Rum
  Flaming not recommended

FLORIDA JOYS
Shake and Strain
  1 oz Vodka
  1/2 oz Triple Sec
  Splash Orange,
  Grapefruit Juice

FRENCH TICKLE
Layer
  Cherry Liqueur
  Peach Brandy
  Cream
  Cherry Garnish

FUZZY PRICK
Layer
  Peach Schnapps
  Pineaple Juice

GOLD RUSH
Layer
  Frangelico
  Yukon Jack
  Vodka
  Flaming not recommended

GRAND SLAMMER
Shake and Strain
  1 oz Gin
  1/2 oz Grand Marnier
  Dash Orange Juice
  Grenadine

"*Simply*
SHOOTERS"

GRAPE CRUSH (APE)
Shake and Strain
  1 oz Vodka
  1 oz Blackberry Brandy
  (Grape Juice)
  Splash Sour Mix
  Top With 7-Up

GREENIE MEANIE
Shake and Strain
  Midori
  Southern Comfort
  Pineapple Juice

GUTS
Layer
  Cherry Brandy
  Ouzo
  Irish Cream

HAIROIN'S BAD FO YA!
Layer
  Anisette
  Drops Cherry Brandy
  Cointreau

HAT TRICK
Layer
  Grenadine
  Kahlua
  Bailey's

HORNEY TOAD
Layer
  Kahlua
  Amaretto
  Jack Daniels

IRISH QUAALUDE
Layer
  W. Creme de Cacao
  Frangelico
  Bailey's
  Vodka
  Flaming not recommended

JACK N' OFF
Shake and Strain
  Jack Daniels
  Smirnoff
  Peach Brandy
  Grenadine
  Orange Juice
  Sour Mix

JAMAICA US MAD!
Shake and Strain
  Dark Rum
  Spiced Rum
  Blue Curacao
  Splash Orange,
  Pineapple Juice

JET FUEL
Layer
  Grenadine
  W. Creme de Menthe
  Yukon Jack

"Simply SHOOTERS"

JUICIE LUCIE
Shake and Strain
- 1 1/2 oz Malibu
- 1 oz Pineapple Juice
- 1/2 oz Cranberry Juice

KO CANE'LL GIT YA!
Layer
- Kahlua
- Amaretto
- Tequila
- *Flaming not recommended*

LIGHTER FLUID
Layer
- Drambuie
- Tequila
- Drops of Tabasco

LOUNGE LIZARD
Shake and Strain
- 1 1/2 oz Myers's Dark Rum
- Splash Each: Sour, Orange, Pineapple
- Float Cherry Brandy

M-16
Layer
- D. Creme de Cacao
- B&B

MEISTER BATION
Shake and Strain
- 1 oz Jagermesiter
- 1/2 oz Creme de Banana
- Splash Cream
- Pina Colada Mix

MONKEY SEE AND DO
Layer
- Kahlua
- Banana Liqueur
- Bailey's Irish Cream
- Top with Dark Rum
- *Flaming not recommended*

MONTH AT THE BEACH (MAUI WOWIE)
Shake and Strain
- Dash Each: Vodka, Midori, Peach Brandy, Apple Schnapps
- Orange, Cranberry Juice

MOTHER'S MILK
Layer
- Frangelico
- Malibu
- Cream

STOP THE PRESS! RECIPE ADDENDUM

NUCLEAR SPILL
Shake and Strain
 Equal Parts: Vodka,
 Midori, Peach Brandy,
 Creme de Banana,
 Whip Cream

ORAL SIX
Layer
 Triple Sec
 Bailey's
 Southern Comfort

PANDORA'S BOX
Shake and Strain
 1 oz Vodka
 1/2 oz Triple Sec
 1/2 oz Pineapple Juice

PEACH ON THE BEACH
Shake and Strain
 Vodka, Peach Brandy,
 Orange Juice
 Cranberry Juice

PINK CADDY
Shake and Strain
 1 1/2 oz Rum
 1/2 oz Cherry Brandy
 Dash Pineapple,
 Cranberry Juice

POWER MUD SLIDE
Layer
 Kahlua
 Bailey's
 Jagermeister
 100° Vodka
 Flaming not recommended

POWER SLIDE
Layer
 Kahlua
 Bailey's
 Jagermeister

PURPLE FLIRT
Shake and Strain
 1 oz Dark Rum
 1/2 oz Blueberry
 Schnapps
 1/2 oz Grenadine
 Splash Sour Mix,
 Pineapple Juice

RAZZBALL
Shake and Strain
 1/2 oz Vodka
 1 oz Chambord
 Dash Orange,
 Pineapple Juice

RAZZBERRY QUICK
Rocks Glass, Crushed Ice
 Raspberry Liqueur
 Irish Cream
 Half and Half
 Sip With Straw

STOP THE PRESS! RECIPE ADDENDUM

ROOT CANAL
Layer
Rootbeer Schnapps
151° Rum
Flaming not recommended

SALLY DON'T DANCE MUCH ANYMORE!
Shake and Strain
1 oz Rum
1 1/2 oz Coco Lopez
Splash Pineapple,
Cranberry Juice

SCREAMING LEPRECHAUN
Layer
Bailey's Irish Cream
Vodka
Irish Whiskey

SEX IN THE DIRT
Shake and Strain
Southern Comfort
Amaretto
Creme de Cassis
Orange Juice

SNOW FLAKES
Layer
Peppermint Schnapps
Malibu

SNOW JOB
Layer
W. Creme de Cacao
Amaretto
Cream

SWALLOW!!
Layer
Anisette
Irish Cream

TERMINATOR
Layer
Sambuca
B&B
G. Chartreuse

VENOM
Layer
Yukon Jack
Squeeze Lime Juice

VIBRATOR
Layer
Bailey's Irish Cream
Southern Comfort

WHIP LASH
Layer
Anisette
Sambuca (Black)

"Simply SHOOTERS"

WILD CHERRY
Shake and Strain
> 1/2 oz Vodka
> 1/2 oz Frangelico
> 1/2 oz Blackberry
> Brandy
> 1/2 oz Cherry Brandy
> 1/2 oz Creme de Cassis
> 1/2 oz Grenadine
> Cherry Garnish
> On Glass Rim

WILD SCREW
Shake and Strain
> 3/4 oz Wild Turkey 101°
> 3/4 oz Vodka 100°
> 3/4 oz Triple Sec
> Splash Orange Juice

WOODY
Shake and Strain
> Vodka
> Southern Comfort
> Amaretto
> Grenadine
> Pineapple Juice

NEW SHOOTER RECIPES

NEW SHOOTER RECIPES

NEW SHOOTER RECIPES

"Simply
SHOOTERS"

NEW SHOOTER RECIPES

"Simply
SHOOTERS"

NEW SHOOTER RECIPES

NEW SHOOTER RECIPES

NEW SHOOTER RECIPES

"*Simply* SHOOTERS"

" Simply

SHOOTERS"

a.k.a

COAST TO COAST
SHOOTER
COLLECTION

FOR QUANTITY PRICES

WRITE:

MR. STIRSTICK AND CO.
2511 EDGEWOOD ROAD
COLUMBUS, GEORGIA
31906